REGENTS CRITICS SERIES

General Editor: Paul A. Olson

SHELLEY'S CRITICAL PROSE

Other volumes in the Regents Critics Series are:

Shelley's Critical Prose

Edited by

BRUCE R. McELDERRY, JR.

UNIVERSITY OF NEBRASKA PRESS · LINCOLN

Publishers on the Plains

UNP

Copyright © 1967 by the University of Nebraska Press
All rights reserved
Library of Congress Catalog card number 66–19856

MANUFACTURED IN THE UNITED STATES OF AMERICA

Regents Critics Series

The Regents Critics Series provides reading texts of significant literary critics in the Western tradition. The series treats criticism as a useful tool: an introduction to the critic's own poetry and prose if he is a poet or novelist, an introduction to other work in his day if he is more judge than creator. Nowhere is criticism regarded as an end in itself but as what it is—a means to the understanding of the language of art as it has existed and been understood in various periods and societies.

Each volume includes a scholarly introduction which describes how the work collected came to be written, and suggests its uses. All texts are edited in the most conservative fashion consonant with the production of a good reading text; and all translated texts observe the dictum that the letter gives life and the spirit kills when a technical or rigorous passage is being put into English. Other types of passages may be more freely treated. Footnoting and other scholarly paraphernalia are restricted to the essential minimum. Such features as a bibliographical checklist are carried where they are appropriate to the work in hand. If a volume is the first collection of the author's critical writing, this is noted in the bibliographical data.

PAUL A. OLSON

University of Nebraska

Contents

Introduction

It can almost be said that Shelley became a critic by accident, for if his friend Thomas Love Peacock had not published "The Four Ages of Poetry" (see Appendix B, p. 158) in 1820, Shelley's one formal essay, "A Defence of Poetry," would never have been written. When we turn to the prefaces of the poems published during his short life, however, and to the letters of his later years, we see that Shelley, like most artists, was a critic by temperament. As reader and as writer he sought to define the purposes of literature and to discriminate between fashion and originality, faulty and effective execution, actual achievement and ideal perfection. Had Shelley lived another twenty years, or even another ten, it is possible that he would have become a major critic.

Shelley's reputation as a critic was at its height when Walter E. Peck's biography of him appeared in 1927.[1] Swinburne's judgment of 1875 that in English lyrical poetry Shelley was "supreme and without a second to his race" might still be repeated without a sense of incongruity. It was proudly remembered that the early Yeats had referred in 1900 to "A Defence of Poetry" as "the profoundest essay on the foundation of poetry in English."[2] A. C. Bradley's essay, "Shelley's View of Poetry,"[3] though studious and discriminating, approached Shelley with reverence, as did Oliver Elton in his influential *Survey of English Literature, 1780–1830*.[4] In 1933, however, T. S. Eliot announced that he could not enjoy

1. Walter E. Peck, *Shelley, His Life and Works* (2 vols.; Boston: Houghton Mifflin, 1927).

2. William Butler Yeats, "The Philosophy of Shelley," in *Ideas of Good and Evil* (Stratford-on-Avon: Shakespeare Head Press, 1908). This essay first appeared in 1900.

3. Andrew C. Bradley, "Shelley's View of Poetry," in *Oxford Lectures on Poetry* (London: Macmillan, 1909).

4. Oliver Elton, *A Survey of English Literature, 1780–1830* (2 vols.; New York: Macmillan, 1912).

Shelley's poetry, and that Shelley's ideas were "ideas of adolescence."[5] Eliot's opinion has been widely, though not universally, accepted.

A reading of Shelley's critical prose is the most direct way of seeing how seriously Mr. Eliot undervalued Shelley. Despite its fragmentary nature, the criticism illuminates not only Shelley's own poetry, but the poetry of his age, and the fundamental nature of poetry itself. Besides the formal "Defence" there are the prefaces to his various works; reviews of works by his friends Hogg, Godwin, and Peacock, and by Mary Shelley; and a considerable body of critical comment in his letters. The prefaces show a rapid growth from the eighteenth-century rhetoric of *Laon and Cythna* (1817) to the genuinely critical perceptions about his literary aims and methods in *Prometheus Unbound* and *The Cenci* only three years later. The reviews, two of them posthumously published, are largely puffery, more interesting as insights into the weak side of his sympathies than as evidence of penetrating critical judgment. Comments in the letters are at once more spontaneous and more discriminating. The passages selected for this volume give comments on such English contemporaries as Wordsworth, Coleridge, Lamb, Southey, Scott, Byron, and Keats, and on such continental writers as Rousseau, Goethe, Ariosto, Boccaccio, Dante, and Calderón. Even the briefest reference to such writers suggests a grasp of the man and his work that makes us wish for more elaborate discussion. Of Rousseau's mind he says that it was "so bright as to cast a shade of falsehood on the records that are called reality." Of Ariosto he remarks: "Where is the gentle seriousness, the delicate sensibility, the calm and sustained energy, without which true greatness cannot be?" The letters approach literature as the habitual concern of a keenly curious and discriminating mind that ranged far and dived deep. The letters to Peacock, Hunt, and above all to Byron, are reminders of the brilliant talk that went on when Shelley and his friends turned from personal difficulties to literature.

It cannot be claimed that Shelley developed a critical system in the formal sense. His chief critical utterances came after he was

5. T. S. Eliot, "Shelley and Keats," in *The Use of Poetry and the Use of Criticism* (Cambridge: Harvard University Press, 1933).

twenty-five, and he died at twenty-nine. Only in "A Defence of Poetry" does he try to state fundamental conceptions, and here his rhetorical brilliance has sometimes been regarded as interfering with the clarity of his logic. A brief analysis of the "Defence" will set in perspective the principles he delineated.[6]

Shelley begins by distinguishing the mind's power of synthesis from its power of analysis: poetry derives not from the mind's logical power, or its power of analysis, but from its capacity to synthesize, to see relationships. Synthesizing is thus the essential function of the imagination, and poetry the imagination's essential expression. Rhythm and metaphor are natural to such expression; but other uses of form, sound, and color—even inventions and institutions—may express the poetic impulse. Language, however, is a more plastic medium than other means of expression. After opening his argument, Shelley devotes the early sections of his essay (see pp. 4–26) to the effect of poetry, which is, he says, ever accompanied by pleasure. He compares the poet to the nightingale "who sits in darkness and sings to cheer its own solitude." If pleasure is the first effect of poetry, however, moral improvement is its second; it produces this effect by enlarging man's mind—his capacity for sympathy and love. The historical illustrations of this doctrine with which Shelley supports this view come from the Christian era and from Greek and Roman times, with heavy emphasis of classical drama.

Having argued that poetry improves the moral imagination of mankind, Shelley can insist, in the middle section of his essay (see pp. 26–34), that poetry is superior to science and political philosophy, in part because it derives from a mystical and divine intuition. Indeed, he argues that the poet, when inspired, is not fully accountable, though between moments of inspiration he is a man like other men, subject to the normal human influences, but "more delicately organized." Shelley's final paragraphs of the "Defence" (see pp. 35–36) announce that the second part of the essay will apply the general principles laid down to the "present

6. Albert S. Cook's edition of *A Defense of Poetry* (Boston: Ginn and Company, 1890) has a useful detailed outline of the essay. Cook's spelling of "defense" follows American usage.

state of the cultivation of poetry." This second part, presumably, would have given a more direct reply to Peacock's contention that in modern times the poet is a "semi-barbarian in a civilized community."

It is evident that Shelley's indebtedness to Plato, to Platonic idealism and mysticism, is a central problem. Praising the rhetorical brilliance of the "Defence," M. H. Abrams has pointed out the inconsistency between Shelley's Platonic concept of the mimetic nature of poetry as imitating Platonic ideas and his reference in other passages to the expressive or psychological nature of poetry as a matter of the exercise of the synthetic faculty. If we are to know what the "Defence" says, we must know how Shelley makes a selection from the conflicting doctrines of Plato, and where he abandons Plato to make his own synthesis. One should remember that Peacock's essay, itself an attack on poetry inspired by Plato, found much support for its argument in Plato's banishment of poets from his Republic (Book X), and from a variety of other adverse Platonic comments on poetry (which Shelley ignores): in the *Apology*, for example, Socrates says that poets say many fine things without understanding their meaning; and in the *Phaedrus* poets are ranked below kings, politicians, traders, and even gymnasts. But Shelley, in his essay, ignores this part of Plato, selecting instead favorable views expressed elsewhere. He also ignores Plato's inconsistencies, though it is possible that he intended to deal with them in the parts of the essay which were never written. When he commented on his own translation of *The Banquet* (1818), however, he referred to Plato's "puerile sophisms," and it seems quite likely that he took them into account when he wrote the "Defence." If we follow the sequence of Shelley's argument, looking for echoes of Plato, we may note the following ideas: that poetry is the general power of invention (from the *Symposium* or *The Banquet*); that knowledge is recollection (from the *Phaedo* and the *Meno*); that poetry is a divine inspiration (from the *Ion*, which Shelley translated); that an ideal state would recognize the equality of men (from the *Republic*, Book III); that love "found a worthy poet in Plato alone of all the ancients" (probably a reference to Agathon's long speech in *The Banquet*, which Plato may have intended satirically); and that the poem is an imperfect record of inspiration (from the *Phaedrus*).[7]

One may question, as does Abrams, whether these ideas, in the context of Shelley's argument, are consistent or coherent.[8] Professor Earl R. Wasserman has recently maintained that there is "no inconsistency between Shelley's so-called Platonism and an associational psychology; they complement each other to compose a coherent system."[9] Wasserman accepts as "in some fashion authentic" a dialogue between Byron and Shelley anonymously published in 1830 (see Appendix A, p. 143) and argues from this that Shelley's extended analysis of *Hamlet* in that dialogue is a cogent application of the principles stated in "A Defence of Poetry." Whether the dialogue is accepted as authentic or not, the arguments in it are relevant to the question of whether Shelley achieved in his essay a viable and practically useful conception of poetry. Even before Professor Wasserman's statement of the case, it would have been possible for the sympathetic reader to take Shelley's description of poets and the poetic process as a series of partial truths having an important relevance to an area of discussion which will never be analyzed to the complete satisfaction of all students. That poetry is a creation or invention is true. In relation to its sources, *Hamlet* is not wholly new. Yet when we read or see *Hamlet*, we do have a sense of discovery; poetry seems to awaken the mind to something which has been latent there before. That poetry does accomplish this awakening to the familiar and lost is perhaps the bridge we need to the idea that poetry results from inspiration, for Shelley assumes that inspiration must be received by a temperament sympathetic to it; he rejects Plato's derisive comment to the effect that poets are visited by inspirations which they do not comprehend. Poetry, in his view, is something which the poet cannot will

7. This analysis owes much to Joseph E. Baker's monograph, *Shelley's Platonic Answer to a Platonic Attack* (Iowa City: University of Iowa Press, 1965). The suggestion that the Agathon speech may have been satiric is on p. 24.

8. M. H. Abrams, *The Mirror and the Lamp: Romantic Theory and the Critical Tradition* (New York: Oxford University Press, 1953), p. 129.

9. Earl R. Wasserman, "Shelley's Last Poetics: A Reconsideration," in *From Sensibility to Romanticism*, ed. F. W. Hilles and H. Bloom (New York: Oxford University Press, 1965), pp. 487–511.

to make, but that does not mean that he cannot will to discover it, laid up in the divine mind, or in the realms to which only inspiration has access. If one returns to the distinction laid down in the first paragraph of the "Defence," one may be clearer about the sense in which poetry is invention and the sense in which it is discovery. It is the discovery (or recollection) of an ideal world under the impress of inspiration; it is also the creation of a poetic model of the ideal world (the invention of a poetic model of it) through the combining of objects and impressions seen in time; hence the intrusion of associational psychology. Inspiration works through creation; creation is expression.

The "Defence" may not be a masterpiece of consistent logic, but it is not incoherent. Its most serious shortcoming is its failure to do justice to comedy and its consequent over-insistence on the ideal quality of poetry. There seems to be little room in Shelley's poetic universe for grotesquery and bawdry, for beggarman and thief, or for the worlds of Horace and Juvenal or Terence and Plautus. The blending of comedy with tragedy, as in *King Lear*, Shelley approves; but he says that comedy, as in this play, should be "universal, ideal, and sublime." He views Restoration comedy as the product of a decadent society: "We laugh from self-complacency and triumph, instead of pleasure." Though he emphasizes that the highest drama teaches self-knowledge, in the same paragraph he speaks approvingly of Athenian drama because it strips away "all but that ideal perfection and energy which everyone feels to be the internal type of all that he loves, admires, and would become." Here and elsewhere in the essay, one feels the pressure of a too direct insistence on the presentation of an abstract nobility.

When he viewed actual comic works, however, Shelley was not always limited by the position stated in the "Defence." His statements seem to preclude, for instance, any immediate and favorable response to Byron's *Don Juan*. Yet his first mention of the poem is enthusiastic; in a letter to Peacock, October 8, 1818, he says Lord Byron "read me the first Canto of his 'Don Juan,' a thing in the style of 'Beppo,' but infinitely better." The first two cantos of *Don Juan* were published in July, 1819, and on May 20, 1820, Shelley commented on the printed version. He had reservations:

"I cannot say . . . that I altogether think the bitter mockery of our common nature . . . quite worthy of your genius." Yet the general tone of this letter, and of later comments on *Don Juan*, is highly laudatory. On August 10, 1821, he wrote to Mary: "I despair of rivalling Lord Byron, and there is no other with whom it is worth contending." The intimate friendship between the two men at this period owed something to their common rebellion against British respectability, but Shelley's esteem of *Don Juan* went far deeper than that, as any reader of their correspondence must see. Had Shelley proceeded, as he planned, to discuss the poetry of his contemporaries, his high opinion of Byron's poetry would have led him to qualify his doctrines concerning comic, ironic, and satiric modes of writing. Even his own attempts at satiric poetry, *Oedipus Tyrannus* (1820) and *Peter Bell the Third* (written 1819; published 1839), though not notably successful, illustrate poetic possibilities not sufficiently allowed for in the "Defence."

Critics of Shelley sometimes mock his expressed view, related to his conception of comedy and the ideal, that the poet "ought to be the happiest, the best, the wisest, and the most illustrious of men." One may easily point to Shelley's life and ask, was he happy, good, and wise? The question misconceives Shelley's meaning (though he has certainly stated it clumsily). As a man, a poet is susceptible to all human ills and follies, and Shelley suffered a generous portion of them in his short life. Nevertheless, as a poet, he must have enjoyed, through his insight and creative power, a kind of happiness that few men experience. The distinction is blurred in Shelley's statement, but properly distinguished, the poet's happiness is real. To display Shelley's own virtue and wisdom may require that we make paradoxical distinctions; but virtue and wisdom are godlike attributes, and if the poet is inspired, his inspiration must confer something of virtue and wisdom as well as happiness. If, as Shelley says, the best poems are but a "feeble shadow of the original conceptions," then the lives of poets, too, may be but shadows of the virtue and wisdom they are gifted to perceive.

One may inquire where Shelley's "Defence" comes from: aside from Plato, what are its antecedents? Its very high conception of the office of the poet was developed in the Renaissance tradition, under the influence of the Plato who defended poets, and his Renaissance followers. The poet's prerogatives were never, in that period, assigned more dignity than in Sir Philip Sidney's *Defence of Poesie* (1595), which Mary Shelley was reading at the time Shelley composed his own essay. Sidney, like many other Neoplatonists, accepted Plato's favorable comments on poets and ignored or explained away his derogatory remarks: he described poets as philosophers and as "makers" or creators; he asserted the superiority of poetry to moral philosophy and to history; he answered objections against poetry raised by Stephen Gosson in his *School of Abuse* (1579) by insisting that a knowledge of poetry is as fruitful as any knowledge, that poetic imaginings are not lies, that the abuse of poetry for lustful purposes is no argument against its proper use, and that Plato's proscription of poets from his Republic is merely a condemnation of the abuse of poetry; and he closed with a lament for the low state of English poetry and with a hope for its improvement.

Traditionally, the influence of Sidney on Shelley's "Defence" has been heavily weighted,[10] but it is very likely that Wordsworth's "Preface" to the second edition of *Lyrical Ballads* (1800) was equally influential, and that this would have been made clear in the extension of the "Defence" that Shelley planned but never wrote. Though Shelley does not mention Wordsworth in the essay we have, it is well known that he esteemed Wordsworth's poetry. In a review of Godwin's *Mandeville*, Shelley praises Godwin by equating his influence in moral philosophy to that of Wordsworth as a poet. Wordsworth's "Preface" was so familiar, and so vigorously brought to public attention in 1817 by Coleridge's *Biographia Literaria*, that Shelley could hardly have been ignorant of it. There is surely an echo of Wordsworth in the preface to *The Cenci* when Shelley remarks: "I entirely agree with those modern critics who assert that in order to move men to true sympathy we must use the familiar language of men." Wordsworth's aim, of course, was very different from Shelley's: Wordsworth was justifying a particular class of

10. Albert S. Cook edited Sidney's essay under the title *The Defense of Poesy* (Boston: Ginn and Company, 1890). The fact that he edited both Sidney's and Shelley's essays at about the same time may account in part for his heavy emphasis of Sidney's influence on Shelley.

poetry, while Shelley was justifying poetry itself; Wordsworth gave great attention to the special problem of diction, whereas Shelley provided a brief review of European drama.

Nevertheless, about half of each essay in some degree parallels the other: both Shelley and Wordsworth agree in conceiving the poet as a man differing from other men only by possessing a greater degree of sensibility (since the poet shares the common nature of man he can never be the property of cults); both emphasize the importance of inspiration and minimize the external element of verse (inspired prose is more poetical than uninspired verse); and both emphasize pleasure as a necessary accompaniment of poetry. To both poets, one of the richest sources of pleasure is the imaginative discovery of new similarities, the extension of man's sympathies, and thus of his moral nature. If poetry cannot provide society with a moral code, it can stimulate and purify the feelings which support a vital morality. Thus it has, in an accurate sense, a greater value than science; it is, as Wordsworth says, "the breath and finer spirit of all knowledge," or, in Shelley's words, "at once the center and circumference of knowledge." In making such large claims, no doubt both men owe something to Coleridge and his theory of the creative imagination; but both were also speaking for themselves and for what they thought they, as poets, had done.

Shelley's indebtedness to Plato, Sidney, Wordsworth, and Coleridge does not greatly reduce the originality of his "Defence." He rediscovers old truths and colors them with individual perceptions, analogies, and applications. No one would confuse a paragraph of Shelley's essay with one from Plato, Sidney, Wordsworth, or Coleridge. In their separate ways all of these writers have not merely written about literature; what they have written *is* literature. The "Defence" is the proper introduction to all the rest of Shelley's criticism and to his poetry as well.

In a useful edition of Shelley's prose, Professor David Lee Clark[11] suggests that Shelley's poetry should first be approached through his prose. Though Shelley's best-known lyrics will yield pleasure and meaning without previous preparation, it is certainly true that

11. David Lee Clark (ed.), *Shelley's Prose* (Albuquerque: University of New Mexico Press, 1954).

extended study of his poetry gains greatly from a study of his prose, particularly his critical prose. Shelley's religious and philosophical ideas will often strike a twentieth-century reader as quaint and dated; his ideas on literature are still relevant, particularly as one reads his own poetry.

Shelley's poetry is difficult because it is intense and intellectual and because its intensity and intellectuality are prolonged in passages that strain the reader's attention to the breaking point. The relatively early "Hymn to Intellectual Beauty" (1816) has seven twelve-line stanzas. The last of them begins:

> The day becomes more solemn and serene
> When noon is past—there is a harmony
> In autumn and a lustre in its sky,
> Which through the summer is not heard or seen,
> As if it could not be, as if it had not been!

Detached from its context, this is a simple statement, expressed in familiar words and phrased almost in prose order. The comparison of afternoon to autumn is not, on the surface, difficult; there are no cascades of metaphor here to distract attention, as there are, for example in "Ode to the West Wind" (1820). The words, though separately familiar, in combination are abstract and ideal, and so is the idea which they convey. The harmony of sound, here so subtly modulated by the varied pauses, demands as well as rewards attention; the reader has already followed Shelley through seventy-two lines which develop the contrast between the world of appearance and the reality that lies behind it. What does the unstated comparison of afternoon to autumn mean, and what do both have to do with the conception of Intellectual Beauty? The reader who wishes to get at the technique and meaning of this poem, so central to Shelley's peculiar individuality as a poet, will surely gain from encountering Shelley's explanation of synthesis, intuition, and imagination in "A Defence of Poetry." He will also gain from reading Shelley's remarks on his own poems and on the poems of others.

Few recent poets and few writers of prose in any time approach Shelley in sheer command of the potential harmony of language.

This is true not only in the great lyrics, but also in the more numerous passages of description and exposition which may fairly be called musical speech. Finding the harmony in Shelley, we tend to think of it as ornament, and we set him down as a mere rhapsodist incapable of coherent thought, drifting irresistibly from sense to sound, like Swinburne. Shelley's prose, from the rhetoric of the preface to *Laon and Cythna* to the easy familiarity of the letters, should help us to realize that Shelley was deeply thoughtful by habit, just as he was emotionally sensitive by nature. This is not to say that Shelley was free from error, for being thoughtful is not the same as being "right." There have been few men of genius, however, in whom intelligence and emotion were less at odds. Again and again Shelley's prose shows us how feeling can enliven thought, and how thought can enrich and purify feeling. It was this sense of united powers that Shelley relished most in Greek literature, and that he, as a critic, desired most to transmit and to stimulate in his own time. The fear that this harmony of mind and feeling has been lost is the disease of modern life. It is a compelling reason for a return to Shelley.

One statement in the "Defence" may seem contradictory, and will surely be misleading with regard to Shelley's own poetry. He says: "I appeal to the greatest poets of the present day whether it is not an error to assert that the finest passages of poetry are produced by labor and study." Shelley's notebooks and his manuscripts [12] show abundant evidence of his own labor and study in formulating his seemingly spontaneous lines. When Shelley wrote the essay, however, the rules and the polish of the eighteenth century were still foremost in the minds of critics and readers of poetry. He might have agreed with Pope that "True ease in writing comes from art, not chance," but ease, in the eighteenth-century sense, Shelley did not find satisfying. He venerated in older literatures the substance of imaginative perception, the energy of

12. See, for example, H. Buxton Forman (ed.), *Shelley's Notebooks* (Boston: Bibliophile Society, 1911); Bennett Weaver, "Shelley," in *The English Romantic Poets*, ed. Thomas M. Raysor (New York: Modern Language Association, 1950); and Neville Rogers, *Shelley at Work: A Critical Inquiry* (Oxford: Clarendon Press, 1956).

inspiration. In his own practice, when inspiration came, he was ready to supply the labor of composition, and a critical evaluation of the result.

A Note on the Texts

The texts of "A Defence of Poetry," Shelley's prefaces to his poems, and his five reviews are taken from the Julian Edition of *The Complete Works of Percy Bysshe Shelley*, edited by Roger Ingpen and Walter E. Peck in ten volumes (New York: Charles Scribner's Sons, 1926–1930). This edition has just been reissued by the Gordian Press (Brooklyn, N.Y.: 1965), and thanks are due to Mr. Charles Benevento of that firm for permission to reprint the passages mentioned. The Julian Edition follows closely the original editions; for details of the editorial procedure, see Vol. I, pp. viii–ix. Donald H. Reiman, in his *Shelley's "The Triumph of Life": A Critical Study* (Urbana: University of Illinois Press, 1965), has given a review of the problems of editing Shelley's text (pp. 119–128).

With four exceptions, passages from Shelley's letters are quoted from Roger Ingpen's edition (London: Sir Isaac Pitman and Sons, Ltd., 1909); later editions of these passages show no significant variants. From *Lord Byron's Correspondence* (London: John Murray, 1922) I have quoted from letters by Shelley dated July 9, 1817; May 26, 1820; and April 16, 1821. From *The Works of Lord Byron: Letters and Journals* (London: John Murray, 1901) I have quoted the letter dated October 21, 1821. These letters are all included in the edition of Shelley's letters by F. L. Jones (Oxford: Clarendon Press, 1964).

The text of the anonymous dialogue, "Byron and Shelley on the Character of Hamlet," is reprinted from *The New Monthly Magazine and Literary Journal* of 1830, where it first appeared. Thomas Love Peacock's "Four Ages of Poetry" is reprinted from H. Buxton Forman's *The Works of Percy Bysshe Shelley* (London: Reeves and Turner, 1880), VII, 386–404, which follows closely the original printing of the essay in *Ollier's Literary Miscellany*, 1820.

In the present edition a very few changes in spelling have been made: *Shakespeare* for *Shakspear; enchanted* for *inchanted*. All of Shelley's footnotes have been preserved, except those to the preface of

Hellas, which are omitted since they are wholly historical. Foreign language quotations have been translated in the text; the original words follow, either in brackets or in footnotes. In quoting from Shelley's letters, noncritical comments have frequently been omitted; ellipses, supplied by the editor, indicate such omissions.

BRUCE R. MCELDERRY, JR.

University of Southern California

Shelley's Life and Principal Works

(Dates follow Newman I. White's *Shelley*, 1940 edition.)

1792   Born August 4 at Field Place, near Horsham, Sussex.

1802–1804   At Syon House Academy, near London.

1804–1810   At Eton.

1810–1811   Entered University College, Oxford, in October. Expelled March 25, with his friend Thomas Jefferson Hogg, for publication of an anonymous pamphlet, "The Necessity of Atheism."

1811   Eloped with Harriet Westbrook, August 25; married her in Edinburgh, August 28 or 29. Permanently estranged from his family.

1813   Daughter, Ianthe, born June 28.
            Printed *Queen Mab* in May or June.

1814   Eloped with Mary Wollstonecraft Godwin, July 28. Son, Charles, born to Harriet, November 30.

1816   Son, William, born to Mary, January 24. Traveled in Switzerland and France, May to September. Harriet drowned herself December 10. Shelley and Mary married, December 29.
            Alastor published in February.

1817   Chancery court refused custody of Harriet's children to Shelley, March 27. Daughter, Clara, born September 2.

1818   Settled in Italy in March, living successively in Este, Naples, Rome, Leghorn, Pisa, Lerici. Clara died September 24.
            The Revolt of Islam (originally titled *Laon and Cythna*) published in January.

1819   William died June 7. Percy Florence (surviving heir) born November 12.

Rosalind and Helen published, spring.

1820   *The Cenci* published in March or April; *Prometheus Unbound*, in August; *Oedipus Tyrannus* (anonymously), in December.

1821   Wrote "A Defence of Poetry," February and March.

Epipsychidion published in May; *Adonais* printed in July.

1822   Drowned with Edward Williams, returning from Leghorn, Italy, to Lerici, July 8.

Hellas published in March.

1824   *Julian and Maddalo* included in *Posthumous Poems of Percy Bysshe Shelley*, edited by Mary Shelley.

1839   *Peter Bell the Third* included in *The Poetical Works of Percy Bysshe Shelley* (second edition), edited by Mary Shelley.

1840   "A Defence of Poetry" and translation of Plato's *The Banquet* included in *Essays, Letters from Abroad, Translations and Fragments*, edited by Mary Shelley.

A DEFENCE OF POETRY

A Defence of Poetry

To a new magazine launched in 1820 by the publisher of Shelley's Laon and Cythna, *his friend Thomas Love Peacock contributed "The Four Ages of Poetry," a clever satiric essay maintaining that "a poet in our times is a semi-barbarian in a civilized community" (see Appendix B). On January 20, 1821, Shelley wrote the publishers of the magazine, C. and J. Ollier:*

I am enchanted with your Literary Miscellany, *although the last article it contains has excited my polemical faculties so violently, that the moment I get rid of my ophthalmia I mean to set about an answer to it, which I will send you, if you please. It is very clever, but, I think, very false.*

By February 15, if not before, Shelley knew that Peacock was the author of the essay, for in a letter to Peacock on that date he referred good-naturedly to his desire "to break a lance with you." On March 20, Shelley wrote the publishers:

I send you the Defence of Poetry, Part I. *It is transcribed, I hope, legibly. I have written nothing which I do not think necessary to the subject. Of course if any expressions strike you as too unpopular, I give you the power of omitting them; but I trust you will, if possible, refrain from exercising it. I hope that I have treated the question with that temper and spirit as to silence cavil. I propose to add two other parts in two succeeding Miscellanies. It is to be understood that, although you may omit, you do not alter or add.*

The following day Shelley wrote Peacock to the same effect,

adding: "You will see that I have taken a more general view of what is poetry than you have, and will perhaps agree with several of my positions, without considering your own touched."[1]

Since no further numbers of Ollier's Literary Miscellany *appeared, Shelley planned to publish his essay in* The Liberal, *which Byron, Leigh*

1. *The Letters of Percy Bysshe Shelley,* ed. Roger Ingpen (London: Sir Isaac Pitman and Sons, Ltd., 1909), II, 845–846, 847, 858, 859.

Hunt, and his brother launched in 1822. The Liberal, *too, was short-lived, and when Shelley died the essay was still unpublished. In 1840 it was the first item in* Essays, Letters from Abroad, Translations and Fragments, *edited in two volumes by Mary, his widow. This edition, and most succeeding ones, omitted several direct allusions to Peacock's essay as no longer appropriate or significant after the passage of twenty years. The text which follows, reprinted from the Julian Edition, restores those passages.*

PART I

According to one mode of regarding those two classes of mental action, which are called reason and imagination, the former may be considered as mind contemplating the relations borne by one thought to another, however produced; and the latter, as mind acting upon those thoughts so as to colour them with its own light, and composing from them, as from elements, other thoughts, each containing within itself the principle of its own integrity. The one is the $\tau\grave{o}$ $\pi o\iota\epsilon\iota\nu$, or the principle of synthesis, and has for its objects those forms which are common to universal nature and existence itself; the other is the $\tau\grave{o}$ $\lambda o\gamma\iota\zeta\epsilon\iota\nu$, or principle of analysis, and its action regards the relations of things, simply as relations; considering thoughts, not in their integral unity, but as the algebraical representations which conduct to certain general results. Reason is the enumeration of quantities already known; imagination is the perception of the value of those quantities, both separately and as a whole. Reason respects the differences, and imagination the similitudes of things. Reason is to imagination as the instrument to the agent, as the body to the spirit, as the shadow to the substance.

Poetry, in a general sense, may be defined to be "the expression of the imagination": and poetry is connate with the origin of man. Man is an instrument over which a series of external and internal impressions are driven, like the alternations of an ever-changing wind over an Æolian lyre, which move it by their motion to ever-changing melody. But there is a principle within the human being, and perhaps within all sentient beings, which acts otherwise than in the lyre, and produces not melody, alone, but harmony, by an internal adjustment of the sounds or motions thus excited to the impressions which excite them. It is as if the lyre could accommodate its chords to the motions of that which strikes them, in a determined proportion of sound; even as the musician can accommodate his voice to the sound of the lyre. A child at play by itself will express its delight by its voice and motions; and every inflexion of tone and every gesture will bear exact relation to a corresponding antitype in the pleasurable impressions which awakened it; it will be the reflected image of that impression; and as the lyre trembles and sounds after the wind has died away, so the child seeks, by prolonging in its voice and motions the duration of the effect, to prolong also a consciousness of the cause. In relation to the objects which delight a child, these expressions are, what poetry is to higher objects. The savage (for the savage is to ages what the child is to years) expresses the emotions produced in him by surrounding objects in a similar manner; and language and gesture, together with plastic or pictorial imitation, become the image of the combined effect of those objects, and of his apprehension of them. Man in society, with all his passions and his pleasures, next becomes the object of the passions and pleasures of man; an additional class of emotions produces an augmented treasure of expressions; and language, gesture, and the imitative arts, become at once the representation and the medium, the pencil and the picture, the chisel and the statue, the chord and the harmony. The social sympathies, or those laws from which, as from its elements, society results, begin to develop themselves from the moment that two human beings coexist; the future is contained within the present, as the plant within the seed; and equality, diversity, unity, contrast, mutual dependence, become the principles alone capable of affording the motives according to which the will of a social being is determined to action, inasmuch as he is social; and constitute pleasure in sensation, virtue in sentiment, beauty in art, truth in reasoning, and love in the intercourse of kind. Hence men, even in the infancy of society, observe a certain order in their words and actions, distinct from that of the objects and the impressions represented by them, all expression being subject to the laws of that from which it proceeds. But let us dismiss those more general considerations which might involve an inquiry into the principles of society itself, and restrict our view to the manner in which the imagination is expressed upon its forms.

In the youth of the world, men dance and sing and imitate natural objects, observing in these actions, as in all others, a certain rhythm or order. And, although all men observe a similar, they observe not the same order, in the motions of the dance, in the melody of the song, in the combinations of language, in the series of their imitations of natural objects. For there is a certain order or rhythm belonging to each of these classes of mimetic representation, from which the hearer and the spectator receive an intenser and purer pleasure than from any other: the sense of an approximation to this order has been called taste by modern writers. Every man in the infancy of art, observes an order which approximates more or less closely to that from which this highest delight results: but the diversity is not sufficiently marked, as that its gradations should be sensible, except in those instances where the predominance of this faculty of approximation to the beautiful (for so we may be permitted to name the relation between this highest pleasure and its cause) is very great. Those in whom it exists in excess are poets, in the most universal sense of the word; and the pleasure resulting from the manner in which they express the influence of society or nature upon their own minds, communicates itself to others, and gathers a sort of reduplication from that community. Their language is vitally metaphorical; that is, it marks the before unapprehended relations of things and perpetuates their apprehension, until the words which represent them, become, through time, signs for portions or classes of thoughts instead of pictures of integral thoughts; and then if no new poets should arise to create afresh the associations which have been thus disorganised, language will be dead to all the nobler purposes of human intercourse. These similitudes or relations are finely said by Lord Bacon to be "the same footsteps of nature impressed upon the various subjects of the world" [2]—and he considers the faculty which perceives them as the storehouse of axioms common to all knowledge. In the infancy of society every author is necessarily a poet, because language itself is poetry; and

2. *De Augment. Scient.*, cap. I, lib. iii. [Shelley's note.]

to be a poet is to apprehend the true and the beautiful, in a word, the good which exists in the relation, subsisting, first between existence and perception, and secondly between perception and expression. Every original language near to its source is in itself the chaos of a cyclic poem: the copiousness of lexicography and the distinctions of grammar are the works of a later age, and are merely the catalogue and the form of the creations of poetry.

But poets, or those who imagine and express this indestructible order, are not only the authors of language and of music, of the dance and architecture, and statuary, and painting; they are the institutors of laws, and the founders of civil society, and the inventors of the arts of life, and the teachers, who draw into a certain propinquity with the beautiful and the true, that partial apprehension of the agencies of the invisible world which is called religion. Hence all original religions are allegorical, or susceptible of allegory, and, like Janus, have a double face of false and true. Poets, according to the circumstances of the age and nation in which they appeared, were called, in the earlier epochs of the world, legislators, or prophets: a poet essentially comprises and unites both these characters. For he not only beholds intensely the present as it is, and discovers those laws according to which present things ought to be ordered, but he beholds the future in the present, and his thoughts are the germs of the flower and the fruit of latest time. Not that I assert poets to be prophets in the gross sense of the word, or that they can foretell the form as surely as they foreknow the spirit of events: such is the pretence of superstition, which would make poetry an attribute of prophecy, rather than prophecy an attribute of poetry. A poet participates in the eternal, the infinite, and the one; as far as relates to his conceptions, time and place and number are not. The grammatical forms which express the moods of time, and the difference of persons, and the distinction of place, are convertible with respect to the highest poetry without injuring it as poetry; and the choruses of Æschylus, and the book of Job, and Dante's Paradise, would afford, more than any other writings, examples of this fact, if the limits of this essay did not forbid citation. The creations of sculpture, painting, and music, are illustrations still more decisive.

Language, colour, form, and religious and civil habits of action are all the instruments and materials of poetry; they may be called poetry by that figure of speech which considers the effect as a synonyme of the cause. But poetry in a more restricted sense expresses those arrangements of language, and especially metrical language, which are created by that imperial faculty, whose throne is curtained within the invisible nature of man. And this springs from the nature itself of language, which is a more direct representation of the actions and passions of our internal being, and is susceptible of more various and delicate combinations, than colour, form, or motion, and is more plastic and obedient to the control of that faculty of which it is the creation. For language is arbitrarily produced by the imagination, and has relation to thoughts alone; but all other materials, instruments, and conditions of art, have relations among each other, which limit and interpose between conception and expression. The former is as a mirror which reflects, the latter as a cloud which enfeebles, the light of which both are mediums of communication. Hence the fame of sculptors, painters, and musicians, although the intrinsic powers of the great masters of these arts may yield in no degree to that of those who have employed language as the hieroglyphic of their thoughts, has never equalled that of poets in the restricted sense of the term; as two performers of equal skill will produce unequal effects from a guitar and a harp. The fame of legislators and founders of religions, so long as their institutions last, alone seems to exceed that of poets in the restricted sense; but it can scarcely be a question, whether, if we deduct the celebrity which their flattery of the gross opinions of the vulgar usually conciliates, together with that which belonged to them in their higher character of poets, any excess will remain.

We have thus circumscribed the meaning of the word Poetry within the limits of that art which is the most familiar and the most perfect expression of the faculty itself. It is necessary, however, to make the circle still narrower, and to determine the distinction between measured and unmeasured language; for the popular division into prose and verse is inadmissible in accurate philosophy.

Sounds as well as thoughts have relation both between each other and towards that which they represent, and a perception of the order of those relations has always been found connected with a perception of the order of those relations of thoughts. Hence the language of poets has ever affected a certain uniform and harmonious recurrence of sound, without which it were not poetry, and which is scarcely less indispensable to the communication of its action, than the words themselves, without reference to that peculiar order. Hence the vanity of translation; it were as wise to cast a violet into a crucible that you might discover the formal principle of its colour and odour, as seek to transfuse from one language into another the creations of a poet. The plant must spring again from its seed, or it will bear no flower—and this is the burthen of the curse of Babel.

An observation of the regular mode of the recurrence of this harmony in the language of poetical minds, together with its relation to music, produced metre, or a certain system of traditional forms of harmony of language. Yet it is by no means essential that a poet should accommodate his language to this traditional form, so that the harmony, which is its spirit, be observed. The practice is indeed convenient and popular, and to be preferred, especially in such composition as includes much form and action: but every great poet must inevitably innovate upon the example of his predecessors in the exact structure of his peculiar versification. The distinction between poets and prose writers is a vulgar error. The distinction between philosophers and poets has been anticipated. Plato was essentially a poet—the truth and splendour of his imagery, and the melody of his language, is the most intense that it is possible to conceive. He rejected the measure of the epic, dramatic, and lyrical forms, because he sought to kindle a harmony in thoughts divested of shape and action, and he forbore to invent any regular plan of rhythm which should include, under determinate forms, the varied pauses of his style. Cicero sought to imitate the cadence of his periods, but with little success. Lord Bacon was a poet.[3] His language has a sweet and majestic rhythm, which satisfies the sense, no less than the almost superhuman wisdom of his philosophy satisfies the intellect; it is a strain which distends, and then bursts the circumference of the hearer's mind, and pours itself

3. See the *Filum Labyrinthi* and the *Essay on Death* particularly. [Shelley's note.]

forth together with it into the universal element with which it has perpetual sympathy. All the authors of revolutions in opinion are not only necessarily poets as they are inventors, nor even as their words unveil the permanent analogy of things by images which participate in the life of truth; but as their periods are harmonious and rhythmical, and contain in themselves the elements of verse; being the echo of the eternal music. Nor are those supreme poets, who have employed traditional forms of rhythm on account of the form and action of their subjects, less capable of perceiving and teaching the truth of things, than those who have omitted that form. Shakespeare, Dante, and Milton (to confine ourselves to modern writers) are philosophers of the very loftiest power.

A poem is the image of life expressed in its eternal truth. There is this difference between a story and a poem, that a story is a catalogue of detached facts, which have no other bond of connexion than time, place, circumstance, cause and effect; the other is the creation of actions according to the unchangeable forms of human nature, as existing in the mind of the creator, which is itself the image of all other minds. The one is partial, and applies only to a definite period of time, and a certain combination of events which can never again recur; the other is universal, and contains within itself the germ of a relation to whatever motives or actions have place in the possible varieties of human nature. Time, which destroys the beauty and the use of the story of particular facts, stript of the poetry which should invest them, augments that of Poetry, and for ever develops new and wonderful applications of the eternal truth which it contains. Hence epitomes have been called the moths of just history; they eat out the poetry of it. The story of particular facts is as a mirror which obscures and distorts that which should be beautiful: Poetry is a mirror which makes beautiful that which is distorted.

The parts of a composition may be poetical, without the composition as a whole being a poem. A single sentence may be considered as a whole, though it be found in a series of unassimilated portions; a single word even may be a spark of inextinguishable thought. And thus all the great historians, Herodotus, Plutarch, Livy, were poets; and although the plan of these writers, especially

that of Livy, restrained them from developing this faculty in its
highest degree, they make copious and ample amends for their
subjection, by filling all the interstices of their subjects with living
images.

Having determined what is poetry, and who are poets, let us
proceed to estimate its effects upon society.

Poetry is ever accompanied with pleasure: all spirits on which
it falls open themselves to receive the wisdom which is mingled
with its delight. In the infancy of the world, neither poets themselves
nor their auditors are fully aware of the excellence of poetry: for it
acts in a divine and unapprehended manner, beyond and above
consciousness; and it is reserved for future generations to contemplate and measure the mighty cause and effect in all the strength
and splendour of their union. Even in modern times, no living poet
ever arrived at the fulness of his fame; the jury which sits in judgment upon a poet, belonging as he does to all time, must be composed of his peers: it must be impanneled by Time from the selectest
of the wise of many generations. A Poet is a nightingale, who sits in
darkness and sings to cheer its own solitude with sweet sounds; his
auditors are as men entranced by the melody of an unseen musician,
who feel that they are moved and softened, yet know not whence or
why. The poems of Homer and his contemporaries were the delight
of infant Greece; they were the elements of that social system which
is the column upon which all succeeding civilization has reposed.
Homer embodied the ideal perfection of his age in human character;
nor can we doubt that those who read his verses were awakened to
an ambition of becoming like to Achilles, Hector, and Ulysses: the
truth and beauty of friendship, patriotism, and persevering devotion
to an object, were unveiled to the depths in these immortal
creations: the sentiments of the auditors must have been refined
and enlarged by a sympathy with such great and lovely impersonations, until from admiring they imitated, and from imitation they
identified themselves with the objects of their admiration. Nor let it
be objected, that these characters are remote from moral perfection,
and that they can by no means be considered as edifying patterns
for general imitation. Every epoch, under names more or less
specious, has deified its peculiar errors; Revenge is the naked Idol

of the worship of a semi-barbarous age; and Self-deceit is the veiled Image of unknown evil, before which luxury and satiety lie prostrate. But a poet considers the vices of his contemporaries as the temporary dress in which his creations must be arrayed, and which cover without concealing the eternal proportions of their beauty. An epic or dramatic personage is understood to wear them around his soul, as he may the antient armour or the modern uniform around his body; whilst it is easy to conceive a dress more graceful than either. The beauty of the internal nature cannot be so far concealed by its accidental vesture, but that the spirit of its form shall communicate itself to the very disguise, and indicate the shape it hides from the manner in which it is worn. A majestic form and graceful motions will express themselves through the most barbarous and tasteless costume. Few poets of the highest class have chosen to exhibit the beauty of their conceptions in its naked truth and splendour; and it is doubtful whether the alloy of costume, habit, &c., be not necessary to temper this planetary music for mortal ears.

The whole objection, however, of the immorality of poetry rests upon a misconception of the manner in which poetry acts to produce the moral improvement of man. Ethical science arranges the elements which poetry has created, and propounds schemes and proposes examples of civil and domestic life: nor is it for want of admirable doctrines that men hate, and despise, and censure, and deceive, and subjugate one another. But Poetry acts in another and diviner manner. It awakens and enlarges the mind itself by rendering it the receptacle of a thousand unapprehended combinations of thought. Poetry lifts the veil from the hidden beauty of the world, and makes familiar objects be as if they were not familiar; it reproduces all that it represents, and the impersonations clothed in its Elysian light stand thenceforward in the minds of those who have once contemplated them, as memorials of that gentle and exalted content which extends itself over all thoughts and actions with which it coexists. The great secret of morals is love; or a going out of our own nature, and an identification of ourselves with the beautiful which exists in thought, action, or person, not our own. A man, to be greatly good, must imagine intensely and comprehensively; he must put himself in the place of another and of many others; the pains and pleasures of his species must become his own. The great instrument of moral good is the imagination; and poetry administers to the effect by acting upon the cause. Poetry enlarges the circumference of the imagination by replenishing it with thoughts of ever new delight, which have the power of attracting and assimilating to their own nature all other thoughts, and which form new intervals and interstices whose void for ever craves fresh food. Poetry strengthens that faculty which is the organ of the moral nature of man, in the same manner as exercise strengthens a limb. A Poet therefore would do ill to embody his own conceptions of right and wrong, which are usually those of his place and time, in his poetical creations, which participate in neither. By this assumption of the inferior office of interpreting the effect, in which perhaps after all he might acquit himself but imperfectly, he would resign the glory in a participation in the cause. There was little danger that Homer, or any of the eternal Poets, should have so far misunderstood themselves as to have abdicated this throne of their widest dominion. Those in whom the poetical faculty, though great, is less intense, as Euripides, Lucan, Tasso, Spenser, have frequently affected a moral aim, and the effect of their poetry is diminished in exact proportion to the degree in which they compel us to advert to this purpose.

Homer and the cyclic poets were followed at a certain interval by the dramatic and lyrical Poets of Athens, who flourished contemporaneously with all that is most perfect in the kindred expressions of the poetical faculty; architecture, painting, music, the dance, sculpture, philosophy, and we may add, the forms of civil life. For although the scheme of Athenian society was deformed by many imperfections which the poetry existing in Chivalry and Christianity have erased from the habits and institutions of modern Europe; yet never at any other period has so much energy, beauty, and virtue, been developed; never was blind strength and stubborn form so disciplined and rendered subject to the will of man, or that will less repugnant to the dictates of the beautiful and the true, as during the century which preceded the death of Socrates. Of no other epoch in the history of our species have we records and fragments stamped so visibly with the image of the divinity in man. But it is

Poetry alone, in form, in action, or in language, which has rendered this epoch memorable above all others, and the storehouse of examples to everlasting time. For written poetry existed at that epoch simultaneously with the other arts, and it is an idle enquiry to demand which gave and which received the light, which all, as from a common focus, have scattered over the darkest periods of succeeding age. We know no more of cause and effect than a constant conjunction of events: Poetry is ever found to coexist with whatever other arts contribute to the happiness and perfection of man. I appeal to what has already been established to distinguish between the cause and the effect.

It was at the period here adverted to, that the Drama had its birth; and however a succeeding writer may have equalled or surpassed those few great specimens of the Athenian drama which have been preserved to us, it is indisputable that the art itself never was understood or practised according to the true philosophy of it, as at Athens. For the Athenians employed language, action, music, painting, the dance, and religious institutions, to produce a common effect in the representation of the loftiest idealisms of passion and of power; each division in the art was made perfect in its kind by artists of the most consummate skill, and was disciplined into a beautiful proportion and unity one towards another. On the modern stage a few only of the elements capable of expressing the image of the poet's conception are employed at once. We have tragedy without music and dancing; and music and dancing without the high impersonations of which they are the fit accompaniment, and both without religion and solemnity; religious institution has indeed been usually banished from the stage. Our system of divesting the actor's face of a mask, on which the many expressions appropriated to his dramatic character might be moulded into one permanent and unchanging expression, is favourable only to a partial and inharmonious effect; it is fit for nothing but a monologue, where all the attention may be directed to some great master of ideal mimicry. The modern practice of blending comedy with tragedy, though liable to great abuse in point of practice, is undoubtedly an extension of the dramatic circle; but the comedy should be as in King Lear, universal, ideal, and sublime. It is perhaps the intervention of this principle which determines the balance in favour of King Lear against the Œdipus Tyrannus or the Agamemnon, or, if you will the trilogies with which they are connected; unless the intense power of the choral poetry, especially that of the latter, should be considered as restoring the equilibrium. King Lear, if it can sustain this comparison, may be judged to be the most perfect specimen of the dramatic art existing in the world; in spite of the narrow conditions to which the poet was subjected by the ignorance of the philosophy of the drama which has prevailed in modern Europe. Calderón, in his religious Autos, has attempted to fulfil some of the high conditions of dramatic representation neglected by Shakespeare; such as the establishing a relation between the drama and religion, and the accommodating them to music and dancing; but he omits the observation of conditions still more important, and more is lost than gained by a substitution of the rigidly-defined and ever-repeated idealisms of a distorted superstition for the living impersonations of the truth of human passion.

But we disgress.—The Author of the Four Ages of Poetry has prudently omitted to dispute on the effect of the Drama upon life and manners. For, if I know the Knight by the device of his shield, I have only to inscribe Philoctetes or Agamemnon or Othello upon mine to put to flight the giant sophisms which have enchanted him, as the mirror of intolerable light though on the arm of one of the weakest of the Paladines could blind and scatter whole armies of necromancers and pagans.[4] The connexion of scenic exhibitions with the improvement or corruption of the manners of men, has been universally recognised: in other words, the presence or absence of poetry in its most perfect and universal form, has been found to be connected with good and evil in conduct and habit. The corruption which has been imputed to the drama as an effect, begins, when the poetry employed in its constitution ends: I appeal to the history of manners whether the gradations of the growth of the one and the decline of the other have not corresponded

4. The preceding two sentences alluding to Peacock were deleted by Mary Shelley when the essay was first printed, and are not given in most previous editions. The Julian Edition restores the passage.

with an exactness equal to any other example of moral cause and effect.

The drama at Athens, or wheresoever else it may have approached to its perfection, coexisted with the moral and intellectual greatness of the age. The tragedies of the Athenian poets are as mirrors in which the spectator beholds himself, under a thin disguise of circumstance, stript of all but that ideal perfection and energy which every one feels to be the internal type of all that he loves, admires, and would become. The imagination is enlarged by a sympathy with pains and passions so mighty, that they distend in their conception the capacity of that by which they are conceived; the good affections are strengthened by pity, indignation, terror and sorrow; and an exalted calm is prolonged from the satiety of this high exercise of them into the tumult of familiar life: even crime is disarmed of half its horror and all its contagion by being represented as the fatal consequence of the unfathomable agencies of nature; error is thus divested of its wilfulness; men can no longer cherish it as the creation of their choice. In a drama of the highest order there is little food for censure or hatred; it teaches rather self-knowledge and self-respect. Neither the eye nor the mind can see itself, unless reflected upon that which it resembles. The drama, so long as it continues to express poetry, is as a prismatic and many-sided mirror, which collects the brightest rays of human nature and divides and reproduces them from the simplicity of these elementary forms, and touches them with majesty and beauty, and multiplies all that it reflects, and endows it with the power of propagating its like wherever it may fall.

But in periods of the decay of social life, the drama sympathises with that decay. Tragedy becomes a cold imitation of the form of the great masterpieces of antiquity, divested of all harmonious accompaniment of the kindred arts; and often the very form misunderstood, or a weak attempt to teach certain doctrines, which the writer considers as moral truths; and which are usually no more than specious flatteries of some gross vice or weakness, with which the author, in common with his auditors, are infected. Hence what has been called the classical and domestic drama. Addison's "Cato" is a specimen of the one; and would it were not superfluous to cite examples of the other! To such purposes poetry cannot be made subservient. Poetry is a sword of lightning, ever unsheathed, which consumes the scabbard that would contain it. And thus we observe that all dramatic writings of this nature are unimaginative in a singular degree; they affect sentiment and passion, which, divested of imagination, are other names for caprice and appetite. The period in our own history of the grossest degradation of the drama is the reign of Charles II, when all forms in which poetry had been accustomed to be expressed became hymns to the triumph of kingly power over liberty and virtue. Milton stood alone illuminating an age unworthy of him. At such periods the calculating principle pervades all the forms of dramatic exhibition, and poetry ceases to be expressed upon them. Comedy loses its ideal universality: wit succeeds to humour; we laugh from self-complacency and triumph, instead of pleasure; malignity, sarcasm and contempt, succeed to sympathetic merriment; we hardly laugh, but we smile. Obscenity, which is ever blasphemy against the divine beauty in life, becomes, from the very veil which it assumes, more active if less disgusting: it is a monster for which the corruption of society for ever brings forth new food, which it devours in secret.

The drama being that form under which a greater number of modes of expression of poetry are susceptible of being combined than any other, the connexion of poetry and social good is more observable in the drama than in whatever other form. And it is indisputable that the highest perfection of human society has ever corresponded with the highest dramatic excellence; and that the corruption or the extinction of the drama in a nation where it has once flourished, is a mark of a corruption of manners, and an extinction of the energies which sustain the soul of social life. But, as Machiavelli says of political institutions, that life may be preserved and renewed, if men should arise capable of bringing back the drama to its principles. And this is true with respect to poetry in its most extended sense; all language, institution and form, require not only to be produced but to be sustained: the office and character of a poet participates in the divine nature as regards providence, no less than as regards creation.

Civil war, the spoils of Asia, and the fatal predominance first of the Macedonian, and then of the Roman arms, were so many symbols of the extinction or suspension of the creative faculty in Greece. The bucolic writers, who found patronage under the lettered tyrants of Sicily and Egypt, were the latest representatives of its most glorious reign. Their poetry is intensely melodious; like the odour of the tuberose, it overcomes and sickens the spirit with excess of sweetness; whilst the poetry of the preceding age was as a meadow-gale of June, which mingles the fragrance of all the flowers of the field, and adds a quickening and harmonising spirit of its own which endows the sense with a power of sustaining its extreme delight. The bucolic and erotic delicacy in written poetry is correlative with that softness in statuary, music, and the kindred arts, and even in manners and institutions, which distinguished the epoch to which we now refer. Nor is it the poetical faculty itself, or any misapplication of it, to which this want of harmony is to be imputed. An equal sensibility to the influence of the senses and the affections is to be found in the writings of Homer and Sophocles: the former, especially, has clothed sensual and pathetic images with irresistible attractions. Their superiority over these succeeding writers consists in the presence of those thoughts which belong to the inner faculties of our nature, not in the absence of those which are connected with the external: their incomparable perfection consists in an harmony of the union of all. It is not what the erotic writers have, but what they have not, in which their imperfection consists. It is not inasmuch as they were Poets, but inasmuch as they were not Poets, that they can be considered with any plausibility as connected with the corruption of their age. Had that corruption availed so as to extinguish in them the sensibility to pleasure, passion, and natural scenery, which is imputed to them as an imperfection, the last triumph of evil would have been achieved. For the end of social corruption is to destroy all sensibility to pleasure; and, therefore, it is corruption. It begins at the imagination and the intellect as at the core, and distributes itself thence as a paralysing venom, through the affections into the very appetites, till all become a torpid mass in which sense hardly survives. At the approach of such a period, Poetry ever addresses itself to those faculties which are the last to be destroyed, and its voice is heard, like the footsteps of Astræa, departing from the world. Poetry ever communicates all the pleasure which men are capable of receiving: it is ever still the light of life; the source of whatever of beautiful or generous or true can have place in an evil time. It will readily be confessed that those among the luxurious citizens of Syracuse and Alexandria, who were delighted with the poems of Theocritus, were less cold, cruel, and sensual than the remnant of their tribe. But corruption must have utterly destroyed the fabric of human society before poetry can ever cease. The sacred links of that chain have never been entirely disjoined, which descending through the minds of many men is attached to those great minds, whence as from a magnet the invisible effluence is sent forth, which at once connects, animates and sustains the life of all. It is the faculty which contains within itself the seeds at once of its own and of social renovation. And let us not circumscribe the effects of the bucolic and erotic poetry within the limits of the sensibility of those to whom it was addressed. They may have perceived the beauty of those immortal compositions, simply as fragments and isolated portions: those who are more finely organised, or born in a happier age, may recognise them as episodes to that great poem, which all poets, like the co-operating thoughts of one great mind, have built up since the beginning of the world.

The same revolutions within a narrower sphere had place in antient Rome; but the actions and forms of its social life never seem to have been perfectly saturated with the poetical element. The Romans appear to have considered the Greeks as the selectest treasuries of the selectest forms of manners and of nature, and to have abstained from creating in measured language, sculpture, music, or architecture, any thing which might bear a particular relation to their own condition, whilst it might bear a general one to the universal constitution of the world. But we judge from partial evidence, and we judge perhaps partially. Ennius, Varro, Pacuvius, and Accius, all great poets, have been lost. Lucretius is in the highest, and Virgil in a very high sense, a creator. The chosen delicacy of the expressions of the latter, are as a mist of light which conceal from us the intense and exceeding truth of his conceptions of nature. Livy is instinct with poetry. Yet Horace, Catullus, Ovid, and generally the other great writers of the Virgilian age, saw man and nature in the mirror of Greece. The institutions also, and the religion of Rome, were less poetical than those of Greece, as the shadow is less vivid than the substance. Hence poetry in Rome, seemed to follow, rather than accompany, the perfection of political and domestic society. The true poetry of Rome lived in its institutions; for whatever of beautiful, true, and majestic, they contained, could have sprung only from the faculty which creates the order in which they consist. The life of Camillus, the death of Regulus; the expectation of the Senators, in their godlike state, of the victorious Gauls; the refusal of the Republic to make peace with Hannibal, after the battle of Cannæ, were not the consequences of a refined calculation of the probable personal advantage to result from such a rhythm and order in the shews of life, to those who were at once the poets and the actors of these immortal dramas. The imagination beholding the beauty of this order, created it out of itself according to its own idea; the consequence was empire, and the reward ever-living fame. These things are not the less poetry, because they lack a divine bard.[5] They are the episodes of that cyclic poem written by Time upon the memories of men. The Past, like an inspired rhapsodist, fills the theatre of everlasting generations with their harmony.

At length the antient system of religion and manners had fulfilled the circle of its revolution. And the world would have fallen into utter anarchy and darkness, but that there were found poets among the authors of the Christian and Chivalric systems of manners and religion, who created forms of opinion and action never before conceived; which, copied into the imaginations of men, became as generals to the bewildered armies of their thoughts. It is foreign to the present purpose to touch upon the evil produced by these systems: except that we protest, on the ground of the principles already established, that no portion of it can be imputed to the poetry they contain.

It is probable that the astonishing poetry of Moses, Job, David, Solomon, and Isaiah, had produced a great effect upon the mind

5. "*quia carent vate sacro.*" (Horace's *Odes*, Book IV, 9, 25–28.)

of Jesus and his disciples. The scattered fragments preserved to us by the biographers of this extraordinary person, are all instinct with the most vivid poetry. But his doctrines seem to have been quickly distorted. At a certain period after the prevalence of doctrines founded upon those promulgated by him, the three forms into which Plato had distributed the faculties of mind underwent a sort of apotheosis, and became the object of the worship of Europe. Here it is to be confessed that "Light seems to thicken," and

> The crow makes wing to the rooky wood,
> Good things of day begin to droop and drowse,
> And night's black agents to their preys do rouse.[6]

But mark how beautiful an order has sprung from the dust and blood of this fierce chaos! how the World, as from a resurrection, balancing itself on the golden wings of knowledge and of hope, has reassumed its yet unwearied flight into the Heaven of time. Listen to the music, unheard by outward ears, which is as a ceaseless and invisible wind, nourishing its everlasting course with strength and swiftness.

The poetry in the doctrines of Jesus Christ, and the mythology and institutions of the Celtic[7] conquerors of the Roman empire, outlived the darkness and the convulsions connected with their growth and victory, and blended themselves into a new fabric of manners and opinion. It is an error to impute the ignorance of the dark ages to the Christian doctrines or the predominance of the Celtic nations. Whatever of evil their agencies may have contained sprang from the extinction of the poetical principle, connected with the progress of despotism and superstition. Men, from causes too intricate to be here discussed, had become insensible and selfish: their own will had become feeble, and yet they were its slaves, and thence the slaves of the will of others: lust, fear, avarice, cruelty, and fraud, characterised a race amongst whom no one was to be found capable of *creating* in form, language, or institution. The moral anomalies of such a state of society are not justly to be charged upon any class of events immediately connected with them, and those events are most entitled to our approbation which could dissolve it

6. *Macbeth*, III.ii.50–53.
7. Following current usage, Shelley alludes to northern Europe as "Celtic."

most expeditiously. It is unfortunate for those who cannot distinguish words from thoughts, that many of these anomalies have been incorporated into our popular religion.

It was not until the eleventh century that the effects of the poetry of the Christian and Chivalric systems began to manifest themselves. The principle of equality had been discovered and applied by Plato in his Republic, as the theoretical rule of the mode in which the materials of pleasure and of power produced by the common skill and labour of human beings ought to be distributed among them. The limitations of this rule were asserted by him to be determined only by the sensibility of each, or the utility to result to all. Plato, following the doctrines of Timæus and Pythagoras, taught also a moral and intellectual system of doctrine, comprehending at once the past, the present, and the future condition of man. Jesus Christ divulged the sacred and eternal truths contained in these views to mankind, and Christianity, in its abstract purity, became the exoteric expression of the esoteric doctrines of the poetry and wisdom of antiquity. The incorporation of the Celtic nations with the exhausted population of the south, impressed upon it the figure of the poetry existing in their mythology and institutions. The result was a sum of the action and reaction of all the causes included in it; for it may be assumed as a maxim that no nation or religion can supersede any other without incorporating into itself a portion of that which it supersedes. The abolition of personal and domestic slavery, and the emancipation of women from a great part of the degrading restraints of antiquity, were among the consequences of these events.

The abolition of personal slavery is the basis of the highest political hope that it can enter into the mind of man to conceive. The freedom of women produced the poetry of sexual love. Love became a religion, the idols of whose worship were ever present. It was as if the statues of Apollo and the Muses had been endowed with life and motion, and had walked forth among their worshippers; so that earth became peopled by the inhabitants of a diviner world. The familiar appearance and proceedings of life became wonderful and heavenly; and a paradise was created as out of the wrecks of Eden. And as this creation itself is poetry, so its creators were poets;

and language was the instrument of their art: "The book was the Galeotto [go-between], and he who wrote it."[8] The Provençal Trouveurs, or inventors, preceded Petrarch, whose verses are as spells, which unseal the inmost enchanted fountains of the delight which is in the grief of love. It is impossible to feel them without becoming a portion of that beauty which we contemplate: it were superfluous to explain how the gentleness and the elevation of mind connected with these sacred emotions can render men more amiable, and generous and wise, and lift them out of the dull vapours of the little world of self. Dante understood the secret things of love even more than Petrarch. His *Vita Nuova* is an inexhaustible fountain of purity of sentiment and language: it is the idealised history of that period, and those intervals of his life which were dedicated to love. His apotheosis of Beatrice in Paradise, and the gradations of his own love and her loveliness, by which as by steps he feigns himself to have ascended to the throne of the Supreme Cause, is the most glorious imagination of modern poetry. The acutest critics have justly reversed the judgment of the vulgar, and the order of the great acts of the "Divine Drama," in the measure of the admiration which they accord to the Hell, Purgatory, and Paradise. The latter is a perpetual hymn of everlasting Love. Love, which found a worthy poet in Plato alone of all the antients, has been celebrated by a chorus of the greatest writers of the renovated world; and the music has penetrated the caverns of society, and its echoes still drown the dissonance of arms and superstition. At successive intervals, Ariosto, Tasso, Shakespeare, Spenser, Calderón, Rousseau, and the great writers of our own age, have celebrated the dominion of love, planting as it were trophies in the human mind of that sublimest victory over sensuality and force. The true relation borne to each other by the sexes into which human kind is distributed, has become less misunderstood; and if the error which confounded diversity with inequality of the powers of the two sexes has become partially recognised in the opinions and institutions of modern Europe, we owe this great benefit to the worship of which Chivalry was the law, and poets the prophets.

The poetry of Dante may be considered as the bridge thrown

8. "*Galeotto fù il libro, e chi lo scrisse*" (from Dante, *Inferno*, V, 137).

over the stream of time, which unites the modern and antient World. The distorted notions of invisible things which Dante and his rival Milton have idealised, are merely the mask and the mantle in which these great poets walk through eternity enveloped and disguised. It is a difficult question to determine how far they were conscious of the distinction which must have subsisted in their minds between their own creeds and that of the people. Dante at least appears to wish to mark the full extent of it by placing Riphæus, whom Virgil calls the most just man,[9] in Paradise, and observing a most heretical caprice in his distribution of rewards and punishments. And Milton's poem contains within itself a philosophical refutation of that system, of which, by a strange and natural antithesis, it has been a chief popular support. Nothing can exceed the energy and magnificence of the character of Satan as expressed in "Paradise Lost." It is a mistake to suppose that he could ever have been intended for the popular personification of evil. Implacable hate, patient cunning and a sleepless refinement of device to inflict the extremest anguish on an enemy, these things are evil; and, although venial in a slave, are not to be forgiven in a tyrant; although redeemed by much that ennobles his defeat in one subdued, are marked by all that dishonours his conquest in the victor. Milton's Devil as a moral being is as far superior to his God, as One who perseveres in some purpose which he has conceived to be excellent in spite of adversity and torture, is to One who in the cold security of undoubted triumph inflicts the most horrible revenge upon his enemy, not from any mistaken notion of inducing him to repent of a perseverance in enmity, but with the alleged design of exasperating him to deserve new torments. Milton has so far violated the popular creed (if this shall be judged to be a violation) as to have alleged no superiority of moral virtue to his God over his Devil.[10] And this bold neglect of a direct moral purpose is the most decisive proof of the supremacy of Milton's genius. He mingled as it

9. "*justissimus unus.*" Virgil refers to Riphaeus in the *Aeneid*, II, 426–428; Dante in *Paradiso*, XX.

10. This romantic view of Satan is a misinterpretation of *Paradise Lost*; see also Shelley's preface to *Prometheus Unbound*. That Shelley knew Blake's similar view in *The Marriage of Heaven and Hell* is very unlikely.

were the elements of human nature as colours upon a single pallet, and arranged them in the composition of his great picture according to the laws of epic truth; that is, according to the laws of that principle by which a series of actions of the external universe and of intelligent and ethical beings is calculated to excite the sympathy of succeeding generations of mankind. The Divina Commedia and Paradise Lost have conferred upon modern mythology a systematic form; and when change and time shall have added one more superstition to the mass of those which have arisen and decayed upon the earth, commentators will be learnedly employed in elucidating the religion of ancestral Europe, only not utterly forgotten because it will have been stamped with the eternity of genius.

Homer was the first and Dante the second epic poet: that is, the second poet, the series of whose creations bore a defined and intelligible relation to the knowledge and sentiment and religion and political conditions of the age in which he lived, and of the ages which followed it: developing itself in correspondence with their development. For Lucretius had limed the wings of his swift spirit in the dregs of the sensible world; and Virgil, with a modesty which ill became his genius, had affected the fame of an imitator, even whilst he created anew all that he copied; and none among the flock of Mock-birds, though their notes were sweet, Apollonius Rhodius, Quintus Calaber Smyrnetheus, Nonnus, Lucan, Statius, or Claudian, have sought even to fulfil a single condition of epic truth. Milton was the third epic poet. For if the title of epic in its highest sense be refused to the Æneid, still less can it be conceded to the Orlando Furioso, the Gerusalemme Liberata, the Lusiad, or the Fairy Queen.

Dante and Milton were both deeply penetrated with the antient religion of the civilized world; and its spirit exists in their poetry probably in the same proportion as its forms survived in the unreformed worship of modern Europe. The one preceded and the other followed the Reformation at almost equal intervals. Dante was the first religious reformer, and Luther surpassed him rather in the rudeness and acrimony, than in the boldness of his censures of papal usurpation. Dante was the first awakener of entranced Europe; he created a language, in itself music and persuasion, out of a chaos of inharmonious barbarisms. He was the congregator of those great spirits who presided over the resurrection of learning; the Lucifer of that starry flock which in the thirteenth century shone forth from republican Italy, as from a heaven, into the darkness of the benighted world. His very words are instinct with spirit; each is as a spark, a burning atom of inextinguishable thought; and many yet lie covered in the ashes of their birth, and pregnant with a lightning which has yet found no conductor. All high poetry is infinite; it is as the first acorn, which contained all oaks potentially. Veil after veil may be undrawn, and the inmost naked beauty of the meaning never exposed. A great poem is a fountain for ever overflowing with the waters of wisdom and delight; and after one person and one age has exhausted all its divine effluence which their peculiar relations enable them to share, another and yet another succeeds, and new relations are ever developed, the source of an unforeseen and an unconceived delight.

The age immediately succeeding to that of Dante, Petrarch, and Boccaccio, was characterized by a revival of painting, sculpture, music, and architecture. Chaucer caught the sacred inspiration, and the superstructure of English literature is based upon the materials of Italian invention.

But let us not be betrayed from a defence into a critical history of Poetry and its influence on Society. Be it enough to have pointed out the effects of poets, in the large and true sense of the word, upon their own and all succeeding times,[11] and to revert to the partial instances cited as illustrations of an opinion the reverse of that attempted to be established by the Author of the Four Ages of Poetry.

But poets have been challenged to resign the civic crown to reasoners and mechanists on another plea. It is admitted that the exercise of the imagination is most delightful, but it is alleged, that that of reason is more useful. Let us examine as the grounds of this distinction, what is here meant by utility. Pleasure or good, in a general sense, is that which the consciousness of a sensitive and intelligent being seeks, and in which, when found, it acquiesces.

11. The remainder of the paragraph was deleted by Mary Shelley, and restored in the Julian text.

There are two modes or degrees of pleasure, one durable, universal and permanent; the other transitory and particular. Utility may either express the means of producing the former or the latter. In the former sense, whatever strengthens and purifies the affections, enlarges the imagination, and adds spirit to sense, is useful. But the meaning in which the Author of the Four Ages of Poetry seems to have employed the word utility is the narrower one of banishing the importunity of the wants of our animal nature, the surrounding men with security of life, the dispersing the grosser delusions of superstition, and the conciliating such a degree of mutual forbearance among men as may consist with the motives of personal advantage.[12]

Undoubtedly the promoters of utility, in this limited sense, have their appointed office in society. They follow the footsteps of poets, and copy the sketches of their creations into the book of common life. They make space, and give time. Their exertions are of the highest value, so long as they confine their administration of the concerns of the inferior powers of our nature within the limits due to the superior ones. But whilst the sceptic destroys gross superstitions, let him spare to deface, as some of the French writers have defaced, the eternal truths charactered upon the imaginations of men. Whilst the mechanist abridges, and the political economist combines, labour, let them beware that their speculations, for want of correspondence with those first principles which belong to the imagination, do not tend, as they have in modern England, to exasperate at once the extremes of luxury and want. They have exemplified the saying, "To him that hath, more shall be given; and from him that hath not, the little that he hath shall be taken away." The rich have become richer, and the poor have become poorer; and the vessel of the state is driven between the Scylla and Charybdis of anarchy and despotism. Such are the effects which must ever flow from an unmitigated exercise of the calculating faculty.

It is difficult to define pleasure in its highest sense; the definition involving a number of apparent paradoxes. For, from an inexplicable defect of harmony in the constitution of human nature, the pain

12. The last sentence is restored in the Julian text.

of the inferior is frequently connected with the pleasures of the superior portions of our being. Sorrow, terror, anguish, despair itself, are often the chosen expressions of an approximation to the highest good. Our sympathy in tragic fiction depends on this principle; tragedy delights by affording a shadow of the pleasure which exists in pain. This is the source also of the melancholy which is inseparable from the sweetest melody. The pleasure that is in sorrow is sweeter than the pleasure of pleasure itself. And hence the saying, "It is better to go to the house of mourning, than to the house of mirth."[13] Not that this highest species of pleasure is necessarily linked with pain. The delight of love and friendship, the ecstasy of the admiration of nature, the joy of the perception and still more of the creation of poetry is often wholly unalloyed.

The production and assurance of pleasure in this highest sense is true utility. Those who produce and preserve this pleasure are Poets or poetical philosophers.

The exertions of Locke, Hume, Gibbon, Voltaire, Rousseau,[14] and their disciples, in favour of oppressed and deluded humanity, are entitled to the gratitude of mankind. Yet it is easy to calculate the degree of moral and intellectual improvement which the world would have exhibited, had they never lived. A little more nonsense would have been talked for a century or two; and perhaps a few more men, women, and children, burnt as heretics. We might not at this moment have been congratulating each other on the abolition of the Inquisition in Spain. But it exceeds all imagination to conceive what would have been the moral condition of the world if neither Dante, Petrarch, Boccaccio, Chaucer, Shakespeare, Calderón, Lord Bacon, nor Milton, had ever existed; if Raphael and Michael Angelo had never been born; if the Hebrew poetry had never been translated; if a revival of the study of Greek literature had never

13. Ecclesiastes 7:2. The King James version reads: "It is better to go to the house of mourning, than to go to the house of feasting." Shelley includes a variant of this passage in his review of Godwin's *Mandeville*.

14. I follow the classification adopted by the Author of the *Four Ages of Poetry*; but he was essentially a Poet. The others, even Voltaire, were mere reasoners. [Shelley's note.]

taken place; if no monuments of antient sculpture had been handed down to us; and if the poetry of the religion of the antient world had been extinguished together with its belief. The human mind could never, except by the intervention of these excitements, have been awakened to the invention of the grosser sciences, and that application of analytical reasoning to the aberrations of society, which it is now attempted to exalt over the direct expression of the inventive and creative faculty itself.

We have more moral, political and historical wisdom, than we know how to reduce into practice; we have more scientific and economical knowledge than can be accommodated to the just distribution of the produce which it multiplies. The poetry in these systems of thought, is concealed by the accumulation of facts and calculating processes. There is no want of knowledge respecting what is wisest and best in morals, government, and political economy, or at least, what is wiser and better than what men now practise and endure. But we let "*I dare not* wait upon *I would,* like the poor cat i' the adage." We want the creative faculty to imagine that which we know; we want the generous impulse to act that which we imagine; we want the poetry of life: our calculations have outrun conception; we have eaten more than we can digest. The cultivation of those sciences which have enlarged the limits of the empire of man over the external world, has, for want of the poetical faculty, proportionally circumscribed those of the internal world; and man, having enslaved the elements, remains himself a slave. To what but a cultivation of the mechanical arts in a degree disproportioned to the presence of the creative faculty, which is the basis of all knowledge, is to be attributed the abuse of all invention for abridging and combining labour, to the exasperation of the inequality of mankind? From what other cause has it arisen that these inventions which should have lightened, have added a weight to the curse imposed on Adam? Thus Poetry, and the principle of Self, of which Money is the visible incarnation, are the God and Mammon of the world.

The functions of the poetical faculty are twofold; by one it creates new materials for knowledge, and power and pleasure; by the other it engenders in the mind a desire to reproduce and arrange them according to a certain rhythm and order which may be called the beautiful and the good. The cultivation of poetry is never more to be desired than at periods when, from an excess of the selfish and calculating principle, the accumulation of the materials of external life exceed the quantity of the power of assimilating them to the internal laws of human nature. The body has then become too unwieldy for that which animates it.

Poetry is indeed something divine. It is at once the centre and circumference of knowledge; it is that which comprehends all science, and that to which all science must be referred. It is at the same time the root and blossom of all other systems of thought; it is that from which all spring, and that which adorns all; and that which, if blighted, denies the fruit and the seed, and withholds from the barren world the nourishment and the succession of the scions of the tree of life. It is the perfect and consummate surface and bloom of things; it is as the odour and the colour of the rose to the texture of the elements which compose it, as the form and the splendour of unfaded beauty to the secrets of anatomy and corruption. What were Virtue, Love, Patriotism, Friendship— what were the scenery of this beautiful Universe which we inhabit; what were our consolations on this side of the grave, and what were our aspirations beyond it, if Poetry did not ascend to bring light and fire from those eternal regions where the owl-winged faculty of calculation dare not ever soar? Poetry is not like reasoning, a power to be exerted according to the determination of the will. A man cannot say, "I will compose poetry." The greatest poet even cannot say it: for the mind in creation is, as a fading coal, which some invisible influence, like an inconstant wind, awakens to transitory brightness: this power arises from within, like the colour of a flower which fades and changes as it is developed, and the conscious portions of our natures are unprophetic either of its approach or its departure. Could this influence be durable in its original purity and force, it is impossible to predict the greatness of the results; but when composition begins, inspiration is already on the decline, and the most glorious poetry that has ever been communicated to the world is probably a feeble shadow of the original conception of the Poet. I appeal to the great poets of the present day, whether it be not an error to assert that the finest passages of poetry are produced by labour and study. The toil and the delay recommended by critics, can be justly interpreted to mean no more than a careful observation of the inspired moments, and an artificial connexion of the spaces between their suggestions by the intertexture of conventional expressions; a necessity only imposed by the limitedness of the poetical faculty itself. For Milton conceived the Paradise Lost as a whole before he executed it in portions. We have his own authority also for the Muse having "dictated" to him the "unpremeditated song," and let this be an answer to those who would allege the fifty-six various readings of the first line of the Orlando Furioso. Compositions so produced are to poetry what mosaic is to painting. This instinct and intuition of the poetical faculty is still more observable in the plastic and pictorial arts; a great statue or picture grows under the power of the artist as a child in the mother's womb; and the very mind which directs the hands in formation is incapable of accounting to itself for the origin, the gradations, or the media of the process.

Poetry is the record of the best and happiest moments of the happiest and best minds. We are aware of evanescent visitations of thought and feeling sometimes associated with place or person, sometimes regarding our own mind alone, and always arising unforeseen and departing unbidden, but elevating and delightful beyond all expression: so that even in the desire and the regret they leave, there cannot but be pleasure, participating as it does in the nature of its object. It is as it were the interpenetration of a diviner nature through our own; but its footsteps are like those of a wind over a sea, which the coming calm erases, and whose traces remain only, as on the wrinkled sand which paves it. These and corresponding conditions of being are experienced principally by those of the most delicate sensibility and the most enlarged imagination; and the state of mind produced by them is at war with every base desire. The enthusiasm of virtue, love, patriotism, and friendship, is essentially linked with these emotions; and whilst they last, self appears as what it is, an atom to a Universe. Poets are not only subject to these experiences as spirits of the most refined organisation, but they can colour all that they combine with the evanescent hues of this ethereal world; a word, or a trait in the representation of a scene or a passion, will touch the enchanted chord, and reanimate, in those who have ever experienced these emotions, the sleeping, the cold, the buried image of the past. Poetry thus makes immortal all that is best and most beautiful in the world; it arrests the vanishing apparitions which haunt the interlunations of life, and veiling them, or in language or in form, sends them forth among mankind, bearing sweet news of kindred joy to those with whom their sisters abide—abide, because there is no portal of expression from the caverns of the spirit which they inhabit into the universe of things. Poetry redeems from decay the visitations of the divinity in Man.

Poetry turns all things to loveliness; it exalts the beauty of that which is most beautiful, and it adds beauty to that which is most deformed; it marries exultation and horror, grief and pleasure, eternity and change; it subdues to union under its light yoke, all irreconcilable things. It transmutes all that it touches, and every form moving within the radiance of its presence is changed by wondrous sympathy to an incarnation of the spirit which it breathes; its secret alchemy turns to potable gold the poisonous waters which flow from death through life; it strips the veil of familiarity from the world, and lays bare the naked and sleeping beauty, which is the spirit of its forms.

All things exist as they are perceived; at least in relation to the percipient. "The mind is its own place, and of itself can make a Heaven of Hell, a Hell of Heaven." But poetry defeats the curse which binds us to be subjected to the accident of surrounding impressions. And whether it spreads its own figured curtain, or withdraws life's dark veil from before the scene of things, it equally creates for us a being within our being. It makes us the inhabitants of a world to which the familiar world is a chaos. It reproduces the common Universe of which we are portions and percipients, and it purges from our inward sight the film of familiarity which obscures from us the wonder of our being. It compels us to feel that which we perceive, and to imagine that which we know. It creates anew the universe, after it has been annihilated in our minds by the recurrence of impressions blunted by reiteration. It justifies that bold and true

word of Tasso: "None merits the name of creator except God and
the poet." [15]

A poet, as he is the author to others of the highest wisdom,
pleasure, virtue and glory, so he ought personally to be the happiest,
the best, the wisest, and the most illustrious of men. As to his glory,
let Time be challenged to declare whether the fame of any other
institutor of human life be comparable to that of a poet. That he is
the wisest, the happiest, and the best, inasmuch as he is a poet, is
equally incontrovertible: the greatest Poets have been men of the
most spotless virtue, of the most consummate prudence, and, if we
could look into the interior of their lives, the most fortunate of men:
and the exceptions, as they regard those who possessed the imaginative faculty in a high yet inferior degree, will be found on consideration to confirm rather than destroy the rule. Let us for a moment
stoop to the arbitration of popular breath, and usurping and uniting
in our own persons the incompatible characters of accuser, witness,
judge and executioner, let us without trial, testimony, or form,
determine that certain motives of those who are "there sitting where
we dare not soar," [16] are reprehensible. Let us assume that Homer
was a drunkard, that Virgil was a flatterer, that Horace was a coward,
that Tasso was a madman, that Lord Bacon was a peculator, that
Raphael was a libertine, that Spenser was a poet laureate. It is inconsistent with this division of our subject to cite living poets, but Posterity
has done ample justice to the great names now referred to. Their
errors have been weighed and found to have been dust in the balance;
if their sins were as scarlet, they are now white as snow: they have been
washed in the blood of the mediator and the redeemer, Time.
Observe in what a ludicrous chaos the imputations of real or fictitious
crime have been confused in the contemporary calumnies against
poetry and poets; consider how little is, as it appears—or appears,
as it is; look to your own motives, and judge not, lest ye be judged.

Poetry, as has been said, in this respect differs from logic, that
it is not subject to the controul of the active powers of the mind,

15. "*Non merita nome di creatore, se non Iddio ed il Poeta.*" Cf. the reference to the
same passage in Shelley's letter to Peacock, August 16, 1818, pp. 121–122 of this
volume.
16. Adapted from *Paradise Lost*, IV, 829.

and that its birth and recurrence has no necessary connexion with consciousness or will. It is presumptuous to determine that these are the necessary conditions of all mental causation, when mental effects are experienced insusceptible of being referred to them. The frequent recurrence of the poetical power, it is obvious to suppose, may produce in the mind an habit of order and harmony correlative with its own nature and with its effects upon other minds. But in the intervals of inspiration, and they may be frequent without being durable, a Poet becomes a man, and is abandoned to the sudden reflux of the influences under which others habitually live. But as he is more delicately organized than other men, and sensible to pain and pleasure, both his own and that of others, in a degree unknown to them, he will avoid the one and pursue the other with an ardour proportioned to this difference. And he renders himself obnoxious to calumny, when he neglects to observe the circumstances under which these objects of universal pursuit and flight have disguised themselves in one another's garments.

But there is nothing necessarily evil in this error, and thus cruelty, envy, revenge, avarice, and the passions purely evil, have never formed any portion of the popular imputations on the lives of poets.

I have thought it most favourable to the cause of truth to set down these remarks according to the order in which they were suggested to my mind, by a consideration of the subject itself, instead of following that of the treatise that excited me to make them public. Thus although devoid of the formality of a polemical reply; if the view they contain be just, they will be found to involve a refutation of the doctrines of the Four Ages of Poetry, so far at least as regards the first division of the subject. I can readily conjecture what should have moved the gall of the learned and intelligent author of that paper; I confess myself, like him, unwilling to be stunned by the Theseids of the hoarse Codri of the day. Bavius and Mævius undoubtedly are, as they ever were, insufferable persons. But it belongs to a philosophical critic to distinguish rather than confound.[17]

17. Codrus is satirically referred to as the author of a play about Theseus, in *Satires* I, 1–2. Bavius and Maevius are satirically referred to by Virgil, *Eclogues* III, 90, and by Horace, *Epode* 10. In this paragraph the Julian text restores MS readings.

The first part of these remarks has related to Poetry in its elements and principles; and it has been shewn, as well as the narrow limits assigned them would permit, that what is called poetry, in a restricted sense, has a common source with all other forms of order and of beauty, according to which the materials of human life are susceptible of being arranged, and which is Poetry in an universal sense.

The second part will have for its object an application of these principles to the present state of the cultivation of Poetry, and a defence of the attempt to idealize the modern forms of manners and opinions, and compel them into a subordination to the imaginative and creative faculty. For the literature of England, an energetic development of which has ever preceded or accompanied a great and free development of the national will, has arisen as it were from a new birth. In spite of the low-thoughted envy which would undervalue contemporary merit, our own will be a memorable age in intellectual achievements, and we live among such philosophers and poets as surpass beyond comparison any who have appeared since the last national struggle for civil and religious liberty. The most unfailing herald, companion, and follower of the awakening of a great people to work a beneficial change in opinion or institution, is Poetry. At such periods there is an accumulation of the power of communicating and receiving intense and impassioned conceptions respecting man and nature. The persons in whom this power resides, may often as far as regards many portions of their nature, have little apparent correspondence with that spirit of good of which they are the ministers. But even whilst they deny and abjure, they are yet compelled to serve, the Power which is seated upon the throne of their own soul. It is impossible to read the compositions of the most celebrated writers of the present day without being startled with the electric life which burns within their words. They measure the circumference and sound the depths of human nature with a comprehensive and all-penetrating spirit, and they are themselves perhaps the most sincerely astonished at its manifestations; for it is less their spirit than the spirit of the age. Poets are the hierophants of an unapprehended inspiration; the mirrors of the gigantic shadows which futurity casts upon the present; the words which express what they understand not; the trumpets which sing to battle, and feel not what they inspire; the influence which is moved not, but moves. Poets are the unacknowledged legislators of the world.[18]

FRAGMENTS [19]

Probably connected with *A Defence of Poetry*,
and a part of the original exordium.

In one mode of considering these two classes of action of the human mind which are called reason and imagination, the former may be considered as mind employed upon the relations borne by one thought to another, however produced, and imagination as mind combining the elements of thought itself. It has been termed the power of association; and on an accurate anatomy of the functions of the mind, it would be difficult to assign any other origin to the mass of what we perceive and know than this power. Association is, however, rather a law according to which this power is exerted than the power itself; in the same manner as gravitation is a passive expression of the reciprocal tendency of heavy bodies towards their respective centres. Were these bodies conscious of such a tendency, the name which they would assign to that consciousness would express the cause of gravitation; and it were a vain inquiry as to what might be the cause of that cause. Association bears the same relation to imagination as a mode to a source of action: when we look upon shapes in the fire or the clouds and imagine to ourselves the resemblance of familiar objects, we do no more than seize the relation of certain points of visible objects, and fill up, blend together . . . .

18. Much of the last paragraph corresponds with the conclusion of the first chapter of Shelley's *A Philosophical View of Reform*, written in 1820. The last sentence is identical in both texts. See David Lee Clark (ed.), *Shelley's Prose* (Albuquerque: University of New Mexico Press, 1954), p. 240.

19. These fragments were first printed by Dr. Richard Garnett in *Relics of Shelley* (1862), pp. 88–89. Andre H. Koszul thinks the second and third fragments relate to p. 26, beginning "But poets . . . ." For other passages related to the essay, see three drafts of a letter to Ollier, March, 1821, given in *The Letters of Percy Bysshe Shelley*, ed. F. L. Jones (2 vols.; Oxford: Oxford University Press, 1964), II, 272–274.

The imagination is a faculty not less imperial and essential to the happiness and dignity of the human being, than the reason.

It is by no means indisputable that what is true, or rather that which the disciples of a certain mechanical and superficial philosophy call true, is more excellent than the beautiful.

The Complete Works of Percy Bysshe Shelley, ed. Roger Ingpen and Walter E. Peck (Julian Edition, 10 vols.; New York: Charles Scribner's Sons, 1926–1930), VII, 107, 109–140.

PREFACES

Preface to
Alastor; or, The Spirit of Solitude

Alastor *was composed in the autumn of 1815. The preface is overtly didactic, though it is touched with a deeper eloquence than is found in the shrill footnotes of* Queen Mab *(1813), which carried no preface. The final paragraph on the fragment "The Daemon of the World" does not appear in many reprintings of the poem* Alastor. *"The Daemon of the World," published with* Alastor *in 1816, is a revision of sections one and two of* Queen Mab.

[I was not in love as yet, yet I loved to be in love, (and with a more secret kind of want, I hated myself having little want). I sought about for something to love, loving still to be in love.][1]

The poem entitled "Alastor," may be considered as allegorical of one of the most interesting situations of the human mind. It represents a youth of uncorrupted feelings and adventurous genius led forth by an imagination inflamed and purified through familiarity with all that is excellent and majestic, to the contemplation of the universe. He drinks deep of the fountains of knowledge, and is still insatiate. The magnificence and beauty of the external world sinks profoundly into the frame of his conceptions, and affords to their modifications a variety not to be exhausted. So long as it is possible for his desires to point towards objects thus infinite and

---

1. The passage is found at the beginning of the third book of St. Augustine's *Confessions*. The translation above is that by William Watts (1631) in the Loeb Classical Library text (London: William Heinemann, 1912), II, 99. The clause omitted by Shelley is indicated in the translation above by parentheses, and in the Latin by brackets: "*nondum amabam, et amare amabam, [et secretiore indigentia oderam me minus indigentem.] quaerebam quid amarem, amans amare.*"

unmeasured, he is joyous, and tranquil, and self-possessed. But the period arrives when these objects cease to suffice. His mind is at length suddenly awakened and thirsts for intercourse with an intelligence similar to itself. He images to himself the Being whom he loves. Conversant with speculations of the sublimest and most perfect natures, the vision in which he embodies his own imaginations unites all of wonderful, or wise, or beautiful, which the poet, the philosopher, or the lover could depicture. The intellectual faculties, the imagination, the functions of sense, have their respective requisitions on the sympathy of corresponding powers in other human beings. The Poet is represented as uniting these requisitions, and attaching them to a single image. He seeks in vain for a prototype of his conception. Blasted by his disappointment, he descends to an untimely grave.

The picture is not barren of instruction to actual men. The Poet's self-centred seclusion was avenged by the furies of an irresistible passion pursuing him to speedy ruin. But that Power which strikes the luminaries of the world with sudden darkness and extinction, by awakening them to too exquisite a perception of its influences, dooms to a slow and poisonous decay those meaner spirits that dare to abjure its dominion. Their destiny is more abject and inglorious as their delinquency is more contemptible and pernicious. They who, deluded by no generous error, instigated by no sacred thirst of doubtful knowledge, duped by no illustrious superstition, loving nothing on this earth, and cherishing no hopes beyond, yet keep aloof from sympathies with their kind, rejoicing neither in human joy nor mourning with human grief; these, and such as they, have their apportioned curse. They languish, because none feel with them their common nature. They are morally dead. They are neither friends, nor lovers, nor fathers, nor citizens of the world, nor benefactors of their country. Among those who attempt to exist without human sympathy, the pure and tender-hearted perish through the intensity and passion of their search after its communities, when the vacancy of their spirit suddenly makes itself felt. All else, selfish, blind, and torpid, are those unforeseeing multitudes who constitute, together with their own, the lasting misery and loneliness of the world. Those who love not their fellow-beings, live unfruitful lives, and prepare for their old age a miserable grave.

> The good die first,
> And those whose hearts are dry as summer's dust,
> Burn to the socket![2]

The Fragment, entitled "The Dæmon of the World," is a detached part of a poem which the author does not intend for publication. The metre in which it is composed is that of Samson Agonistes and the Italian pastoral drama, and may be considered as the natural measure into which poetical conceptions expressed in harmonious language necessarily fall.

December 14, 1815.

The Complete Works of Percy Bysshe Shelley, ed. Roger Ingpen and Walter E. Peck (Julian Edition, 10 vols.; New York: Charles Scribner's Sons, 1926–1930), I, 173–174.

2. Wordsworth, *The Excursion*, I, 500–502. Wordsworth wrote "they whose hearts."

Preface to
Laon and Cythna

Laon and Cythna *was composed in the summer of 1817. In the autumn it was printed, but the publishers, C. and J. Ollier, refused to release it until some revisions were made; a few copies of the early version survive. Revised and retitled* The Revolt of Islam, *the poem was published in January, 1818. The final paragraph of the original preface, given here, was deleted from the preface to* The Revolt of Islam. *In presenting the poem to his readers, Shelley is chiefly concerned with its revolutionary ideas. He does, however, regard the poem as experimental in a literary sense. He has "avoided imitation of any contemporary style," but he recognizes that his experience contains elements common to his generation. He has chosen the Spenserian stanza as less demanding than blank verse. And he calls for a new criticism, one that is creative, and not enslaved by tradition.*

The Poem which I now present to the world, is an attempt from which I scarcely dare to expect success, and in which a writer of established fame might fail without disgrace. It is an experiment on the temper of the public mind, as to how far a thirst for a happier condition of moral and political society survives, among the enlightened and refined, the tempests which have shaken the age in which we live. I have sought to enlist the harmony of metrical language, the etherial combinations of the fancy, the rapid and subtle transitions of human passion, all those elements which essentially compose a Poem, in the cause of a liberal and comprehensive morality: and in the view of kindling within the bosoms of my readers, a virtuous enthusiasm for those doctrines of liberty and justice, that faith and hope in something good, which neither violence, nor misrepresentation, nor prejudice, can ever totally extinguish among mankind.

For this purpose I have chosen a story of human passion in its most universal character, diversified with moving and romantic adventures, and appealing, in contempt of all artificial opinions or institutions, to the common sympathies of every human breast. I have made no attempt to recommend the motives which I would substitute for those at present governing mankind by methodical and systematic argument. I would only awaken the feelings, so that the reader should see the beauty of true virtue, and be incited to those inquiries which have led to my moral and political creed, and that of some of the sublimest intellects in the world. The Poem, therefore (with the exception of the first Canto, which is purely introductory), is narrative, not didactic. It is a succession of pictures illustrating the growth and progress of individual mind aspiring after excellence, and devoted to the love of mankind; its influence in refining and making pure the most daring and uncommon impulses of the imagination, the understanding, and the senses; its impatience at "all the oppressions which are done under the sun"; its tendency to awaken public hope and to enlighten and improve mankind; the rapid effects of the application of that tendency; the awakening of an immense nation from their slavery and degradation to a true sense of moral dignity and freedom; the bloodless dethronement of their oppressors, and the unveiling of the religious frauds by which they had been deluded into submission; the tranquillity of successful patriotism, and the universal toleration and benevolence of true philanthropy; the treachery and barbarity of hired soldiers; vice not the object of punishment and hatred, but kindness and pity; the faithlessness of tyrants; the confederacy of the Rulers of the World,[1] and the restoration of the expelled Dynasty by foreign arms; the massacre and extermination of the Patriots, and the victory of established power; the consequences of legitimate despotism, civil war, famine, plague, superstition, and an utter extinction of the domestic affections; the judicial murder of the advocates of Liberty; the temporary triumph of oppression, that secure earnest of its final and inevitable fall; the transient nature of ignorance and error, and the eternity of genius and virtue. Such is

1. A reference to the Holy Alliance, formed shortly after the defeat of Napoleon and soon notorious for its tyranny.

the series of delineations of which the Poem consists. And if the lofty passions with which it has been my scope to distinguish this story, shall not excite in the reader a generous impulse, an ardent thirst for excellence, an interest profound and strong, such as belongs to no meaner desires—let not the failure be imputed to a natural unfitness for human sympathy in these sublime and animating themes. It is the business of the Poet to communicate to others the pleasure and the enthusiasm arising out of those images and feelings, in the vivid presence of which within his own mind, consists at once his inspiration and his reward.

The panic which, like an epidemic transport, seized upon all classes of men during the excesses consequent upon the French Revolution, is gradually giving place to sanity. It has ceased to be believed, that whole generations of mankind ought to consign themselves to a hopeless inheritance of ignorance and misery, because a nation of men who had been dupes and slaves for centuries, were incapable of conducting themselves with the wisdom and tranquillity of freemen so soon as some of their fetters were partially loosened. That their conduct could not have been marked by any other characters than ferocity and thoughtlessness, is the historical fact from which liberty derives all its recommendations, and falsehood the worst features of its deformity. There is a reflux in the tide of human things which bears the shipwrecked hopes of men into a secure haven, after the storms are past. Methinks, those who now live have survived an age of despair.

The French Revolution may be considered as one of those manifestations of a general state of feeling among civilized mankind, produced by a defect of correspondence between the knowledge existing in society and the improvement or gradual abolition of political institutions. The year 1788 may be assumed as the epoch of one of the most important crises produced by this feeling. The sympathies connected with that event extended to every bosom. The most generous and amiable natures were those which participated the most extensively in these sympathies. But such a degree of unmingled good was expected, as it was impossible to realize. If the Revolution had been in every respect prosperous, then misrule and superstition would lose half their claims to our abhorrence, as fetters which the captive can unlock with the slightest motion of his fingers, and which do not eat with poisonous rust into the soul. The revulsion occasioned by the atrocities of the demagogues and the re-establishment of successive tyrannies in France was terrible, and felt in the remotest corner of the civilized world. Could they listen to the plea of reason who had groaned under the calamities of a social state, according to the provisions of which, one man riots in luxury whilst another famishes for want of bread. Can he who the day before was a trampled slave, suddenly become liberal-minded, forbearing, and independent? This is the consequence of the habits of a state of society to be produced by resolute perseverance and indefatigable hope, and long-suffering and long believing courage, and the systematic efforts of generations of men of intellect and virtue. Such is the lesson which experience teaches now. But on the first reverses of hope in the progress of French liberty, the sanguine eagerness for good overleapt the solution of these questions, and for a time extinguished itself in the unexpectedness of their result. Thus many of the most ardent and tender-hearted of the worshippers of public good have been morally ruined by what a partial glimpse of the events they deplored, appeared to shew as the melancholy desolation of all their cherished hopes. Hence gloom and misanthropy have become the characteristics of the age in which we live, the solace of a disappointment that unconsciously finds relief only in the wilful exaggeration of its own despair. This influence has tainted the literature of the age with the hopelessness of the minds from which it flows. Metaphysics,[2] and enquiries into moral and political science, have become little else than vain attempts to revive exploded superstitions, or sophisms like those[3] of Mr. Malthus, calculated to lull the oppressors of mankind into a security of everlasting triumph. Our works of

2. I ought to except Sir W. Drummond's *Academical Questions*; a volume of very acute and powerful metaphysical criticism. [Shelley's note.]

3. It is remarkable, as a symptom of the revival of public hope, that Mr. Malthus has assigned, in the later editions of his work, an indefinite dominion to moral restraint over the principle of population. This concession answers all the inferences from his doctrine unfavourable to human improvement, and reduces the *Essay on Population* to a commentary illustrative of the unanswerableness of *Political Justice*. [Shelley's note.]

fiction and poetry have been overshadowed by the same infectious gloom. But mankind appear to me to be emerging from their trance. I am aware, methinks, of a slow, gradual, silent change. In that belief I have composed the following Poem.

I do not presume to enter into competition with our greatest contemporary Poets. Yet I am unwilling to tread in the footsteps of any who have preceded me. I have sought to avoid the imitation of any style of language or versification peculiar to the original minds of which it is the character, designing that even if what I have produced be worthless, it should still be properly my own. Nor have I permitted any system relating to mere words, to divert the attention of the reader from whatever interest I may have succeeded in creating, to my own ingenuity in contriving to disgust them according to the rules of criticism. I have simply clothed my thoughts in what appeared to me the most obvious and appropriate language. A person familiar with nature, and with the most celebrated productions of the human mind, can scarcely err in following the instinct, with respect to selection of language, produced by that familiarity.

There is an education peculiarly fitted for a Poet, without which, genius and sensibility can hardly fill the circle of their capacities. No education indeed can entitle to this appellation a dull and unobservant mind, or one, though neither dull nor unobservant, in which the channels of communication between thought and expression have been obstructed or closed. How far it is my fortune to belong to either of the latter classes, I cannot know. I aspire to be something better. The circumstances of my accidental education have been favourable to this ambition. I have been familiar from boyhood with mountains and lakes, and the sea, and the solitude of forests: Danger, which sports upon the brink of precipices, has been my playmate. I have trodden the glaciers of the Alps, and lived under the eye of Mont Blanc. I have been a wanderer among distant fields. I have sailed down mighty rivers, and seen the sun rise and set, and the stars come forth, whilst I have sailed night and day down a rapid stream among mountains. I have seen populous cities, and have watched the passions which rise and spread, and sink and change, amongst assembled multitudes of men. I have seen the

theatre of the more visible ravages of tyranny and war, cities and
villages reduced to scattered groups of black and roofless houses, and
the naked inhabitants sitting famished upon their desolated thres-
holds. I have conversed with living men of genius. The poetry of
antient Greece and Rome, and modern Italy, and our own country,
has been to me like external nature, a passion and an enjoyment.
Such are the sources from which the materials for the imagery of
my Poem have been drawn. I have considered Poetry in its most
comprehensive sense, and have read the Poets and the Historians,
and the Metaphysicians[4] whose writings have been accessible to
me, and have looked upon the beautiful and majestic scenery of the
earth as common sources of those elements which it is the province
of the Poet to embody and combine. Yet the experience and the
feelings to which I refer, do not in themselves constitute men Poets,
but only prepare them to be the auditors of those who are. How far
I shall be found to possess that more essential attribute of Poetry,
the power of awakening in others sensations like those which animate
my own bosom, is that which, to speak sincerely, I know not; and
which with an acquiescent and contented spirit, I expect to be
taught by the effect which I shall produce upon those whom I now
address.

I have avoided, as I have said before, the imitation of any contemporary style. But there must be a resemblance which does not
depend upon their own will, between all the writers of any particular age. They cannot escape from subjection to a common
influence which arises out of an infinite combination of circumstances belonging to the times in which they live, though each is
in a degree the author of the very influence by which his being is
thus pervaded. Thus, the tragic Poets of the age of Pericles; the
Italian revivers of ancient learning; those mighty intellects of our
own country that succeeded the Reformation, the translators of
the Bible, Shakespeare, Spenser, the Dramatists of the reign of
Elizabeth, and Lord Bacon;[5] the colder spirits of the interval that

4. In this sense there may be such a thing as perfectibility in works of fiction,
notwithstanding the concession often made by advocates of human improvement,
that perfectibility is a term applicable only to science. [Shelley's note.]

5. Milton stands alone in the stage which he illumined. [Shelley's note.]

succeeded;—all resemble each other, and differ from every other in their several classes. In this view of things, Ford can no more be called the imitator of Shakespeare, than Shakespeare the imitator of Ford. There were perhaps few other points of resemblance between these two men, than that which the universal and inevitable influence of their age produced. And this is an influence which neither the meanest scribbler, nor the sublimest genius of any æra, can escape; and which I have not attempted to escape.

I have adopted the stanza of Spenser (a measure inexpressibly beautiful) not because I consider it a finer model of poetical harmony than the blank verse of Shakespeare and Milton, but because in the latter there is no shelter for mediocrity; you must either succeed or fail. This perhaps an aspiring spirit should desire. But I was enticed also, by the brilliancy and magnificence of sound which a mind that has been nourished upon musical thoughts, can produce by a just and harmonious arrangement of the pauses of this measure. Yet there will be found some instances where I have completely failed in this attempt, and one, which I here request the reader to consider as an erratum, where there is left most inadvertently an alexandrine in the middle of a stanza.

But in this, as in every other respect, I have written fearlessly. It is the misfortune of this age, that its Writers, too thoughtless of immortality, are exquisitely sensible to temporary praise or blame. They write with the fear of Reviews before their eyes. This system of criticism sprang up in that torpid interval when Poetry was not. Poetry, and the art which professes to regulate and limit its powers, cannot subsist together. Longinus could not have been the contemporary of Homer, nor Boileau of Horace. Yet this species of criticism never presumed to assert an understanding of its own: it has always, unlike true science, followed, not preceded the opinion of mankind, and would even now bribe with worthless adulation some of our greatest Poets to impose gratuitous fetters on their own imaginations, and become unconscious accomplices in the daily murder of all genius either not so aspiring or not so fortunate as their own. I have sought therefore to write, as I believe that Homer, Shakespeare, and Milton wrote, with an utter disregard of anonymous censure. I am certain that calumny and misrepresentation, though it may move me to compassion, cannot disturb my peace. I shall understand the expressive silence of those sagacious enemies who dare not trust themselves to speak. I shall endeavour to extract from the midst of insult, and contempt, and maledictions, those admonitions which may tend to correct whatever imperfections such censurers may discover in this my first serious appeal to the Public. If certain Critics were as clear-sighted as they are malignant, how great would be the benefit to be derived from their virulent writings! As it is, I fear I shall be malicious enough to be amused with their paltry tricks and lame invectives. Should the Public judge that my composition is worthless, I shall indeed bow before the tribunal from which Milton received his crown of immortality, and shall seek to gather, if I live, strength from that defeat, which may nerve me to some new enterprise of thought which may *not* be worthless. I cannot conceive that Lucretius, when he meditated that poem whose doctrines are yet the basis of our metaphysical knowledge, and whose eloquence has been the wonder of mankind, wrote in awe of such censure as the hired sophists of the impure and superstitious noblemen of Rome might affix to what he should produce. It was at the period when Greece was led captive, and Asia made tributary to the Republic, fast verging itself to slavery and ruin, that a multitude of Syrian captives, bigotted to the worship of their obscene Ashtaroth, and the unworthy successors of Socrates and Zeno, found there a precarious subsistence by administering, under the name of freedmen, to the vices and vanities of the great. These wretched men were skilled to plead, with a superficial but plausible set of sophisms, in favour of that contempt for virtue which is the portion of slaves, and that faith in portents, the most fatal substitute for benevolence in the imaginations of men, which, arising from the enslaved communities of the East, then first began to overwhelm the western nations in its stream. Were these the kind of men whose disapprobation the wise and lofty-minded Lucretius should have regarded with a salutary awe? The latest and perhaps the meanest of those who follow in his footsteps, would disdain to hold life on such conditions.

The Poem now presented to the Public occupied little more than six months in the composition. That period has been devoted to the task with unremitting ardour and enthusiasm. I have exercised a watchful and earnest criticism on my work as it grew under my hands. I would willingly have sent it forth to the world with that perfection which long labour and revision is said to bestow. But I found that if I should gain something in exactness by this method, I might lose much of the newness and energy of imagery and language as it flowed afresh from my mind. And although the mere composition occupied no more than six months, the thoughts thus arranged were slowly gathered in as many years.

I trust that the reader will carefully distinguish between those opinions which have a dramatic propriety in reference to the characters which they are designed to elucidate and such as are properly my own. The erroneous and degrading idea which men have conceived of a Supreme Being, for instance, is spoken against, but not the Supreme Being itself. The belief which some superstitious persons whom I have brought upon the stage entertain of the Deity, as injurious to the character of his benevolence, is widely different from my own. In recommending also a great and important change in the spirit which animates the social institutions of mankind, I have avoided all flattery to those violent and malignant passions of our nature, which are ever on the watch to mingle with and to alloy the most beneficial innovations. There is no quarter given to Revenge, or Envy, or Prejudice. Love is celebrated every where as the sole law which should govern the moral world.

In the personal conduct of my Hero and Heroine, there is one circumstance which was intended to startle the reader from the trance of ordinary life. It was my object to break though the crust of those outworn opinions on which established institutions depend. I have appealed therefore to the most universal of all feelings, and have endeavoured to strengthen the moral sense, by forbidding it to waste its energies in seeking to avoid actions which are only crimes of convention. It is because there is so great a multitude of artificial vices, that there are so few real virtues. Those feelings alone which are benevolent or malevolent, are essentially good or bad. The circumstance of which I speak, was introduced, however, merely to accustom men to that charity and toleration which the exhibition of a practice widely differing from their own, has a tendency to promote.[6] Nothing indeed can be more mischievous, than many actions innocent in themselves, which might bring down upon individuals the bigotted contempt and rage of the multitude.

The Complete Works of Percy Bysshe Shelley, ed. Roger Ingpen and Walter E. Peck (Julian Edition, 10 vols.; New York: Charles Scribner's Sons, 1926–1930), I, 239–247.

6. The sentiments connected with and characteristic of this circumstance have no personal reference to the writer. [Shelley's note.]

Advertisement to
Rosalind and Helen

Rosalind and Helen *was begun in England in 1817, and finished in Italy the following year. It was published in the spring of 1819 as the title poem of a small volume which included "Lines Written on the Euganean Hills," "Hymn to Intellectual Beauty," and the sonnet "Ozymandias." When Shelley speaks in the preface of resigning himself "to the impulse of the feelings which moulded the conception of the story," he is describing what he means in "A Defence of Poetry" by inspiration. The poem illustrates the conception.*

The story of Rosalind and Helen is, undoubtedly, not an attempt in the highest style of poetry. It is in no degree calculated to excite profound meditation; and if, by interesting the affections and amusing the imagination, it awakens a certain ideal melancholy favourable to the reception of more important impressions, it will produce in the reader all that the writer experienced in the composition. I resigned myself, as I wrote, to the impulse of the feelings which moulded the conception of the story; and this impulse determined the pauses of a measure, which only pretends to be regular inasmuch as it corresponds with, and expresses, the irregularity of the imaginations which inspired it.

I do not know which of the few scattered poems I left in England will be selected by my bookseller, to add to this collection. One, which I sent from Italy, was written after a day's excursion among those lovely mountains which surround what was once the retreat, and where is now the sepulchre, of Petrarch. If any one is inclined to condemn the insertion of the introductory lines, which image forth the sudden relief of a state of deep despondency by the radiant visions disclosed by the sudden burst of an Italian sunrise in autumn, on the highest peak of those delightful mountains, I can only offer as my excuse, that they were not erased at the request of a dear friend, with whom added years of intercourse only add to my apprehension of its value, and who would have had more right than any one to complain, that she has not been able to extinguish in me the very power of delineating sadness.

Naples, Dec. 20, 1818.

The Complete Works of Percy Bysshe Shelley, ed. Roger Ingpen and Walter E. Peck (Julian Edition, 10 vols.; New York: Charles Scribner's Sons, 1926–1930), II, 5.

Preface to *The Cenci*

The Cenci was composed from March to August, 1819, printed in Italy, and published in London the following spring. The clear and direct style of the preface contrasts sharply with the rhetorical formality of the preface to Laon and Cythna, *only two years earlier. The story of Beatrice Cenci captured Shelley's sympathy, but also his literary imagination. He sees Beatrice as a tragic character, not as one of merely sentimental appeal. He has consciously avoided "mere poetry," and, echoing Wordsworth, he asserts that to move men "we must use the familiar language of men." Shelley's letter to Peacock, July, 1819 (see pp. 122–124), is an important supplement to the preface.*

DEDICATION

TO

LEIGH HUNT, ESQ.

MY DEAR FRIEND,

I inscribe with your name, from a distant country, and after an absence whose months have seemed years, this the latest of my literary efforts.

Those writings which I have hitherto published, have been little else than visions which impersonate my own apprehensions of the beautiful and the just. I can also perceive in them the literary defects incidental to youth and impatience; they are dreams of what ought to be, or may be. The drama which I now present to you is a sad reality. I lay aside the presumptuous attitude of an instructor, and am content to paint, with such colours as my own heart furnishes, that which has been.

Had I known a person more highly endowed than yourself with all that it becomes a man to possess, I had solicited for this work the ornament of his name. One more gentle, honourable, innocent and brave; one of more exalted toleration for all who do and think evil, and yet himself more free from evil; one who knows better how to receive, and how to confer a benefit, though he must ever confer far more than he can receive; one of simpler, and, in the highest sense of the word, of purer life and manners, I never knew: and I had already been fortunate in friendships when your name was added to the list.

In that patient and irreconcilable enmity with domestic and political tyranny and imposture, which the tenor of your life has illustrated, and which, had I health and talents, should illustrate mine, let us, comforting each other in our task, live and die.

All happiness attend you!

Your affectionate friend,
PERCY B. SHELLEY.

ROME,
May 29, 1819.

PREFACE

A manuscript was communicated to me during my travels in Italy, which was copied from the archives of the Cenci Palace at Rome, and contains a detailed account of the horrors which ended in the extinction of one of the noblest and richest families of that city, during the pontificate of Clement VIII, in the year 1599. The story is, that an old man, having spent his life in debauchery and wickedness, conceived at length an implacable hatred towards his children; which showed itself towards one daughter under the form of an incestuous passion, aggravated by every circumstance of cruelty and violence. This daughter, after long and vain attempts to escape from what she considered a perpetual contamination both of body and mind, at length plotted with her mother-in-law [1] and brother to murder their common tyrant. The young maiden, who was urged to this tremendous deed by an impulse which overpowered its horror, was evidently a most gentle and amiable being,

1. Shelley's use of *mother-in-law* as a synonym for *stepmother* had some currency at the time. See *OED*.

a creature formed to adorn and be admired, and thus violently thwarted from her nature by the necessity of circumstance and opinion. The deed was quickly discovered, and in spite of the most earnest prayers made to the Pope by the highest persons in Rome, the criminals were put to death. The old man had, during his life, repeatedly bought his pardon from the Pope for capital crimes of the most enormous and unspeakable kind, at the price of a hundred thousand crowns; the death therefore of his victims can scarcely be accounted for by the love of justice. The Pope, among other motives for severity, probably felt that whoever killed the Count Cenci deprived his treasury of a certain and copious source of revenue.[2] Such a story, if told so as to present to the reader all the feelings of those who once acted it, their hopes and fears, their confidences and misgivings, their various interests, passions, and opinions, acting upon and with each other, yet all conspiring to one tremendous end, would be as a light to make apparent some of the most dark and secret caverns of the human heart.

On my arrival at Rome, I found that the story of the Cenci was a subject not to be mentioned in Italian society without awakening a deep and breathless interest; and that the feelings of the company never failed to incline to a romantic pity for the wrongs, and a passionate exculpation of the horrible deed to which they urged her, who has been mingled two centuries with the common dust. All ranks of people knew the outlines of this history, and participated in the overwhelming interest which it seems to have the magic of exciting in the human heart. I had a copy of Guido's picture of Beatrice, which is preserved in the Colonna Palace, and my servant instantly recognized it as the portrait of *La Cenci*.[3]

This national and universal interest which the story produces and has produced for two centuries, and among all ranks of people in a great City, where the imagination is kept for ever active and

2. The Papal Government formerly took the most extraordinary precautions against the publicity of facts which offer so tragical a demonstration of its own wickedness and weakness; so that the communication of the MS. had become, until very lately, a matter of some difficulty. [Shelley's note.]

3. The portrait was not by Guido; the real artist has not been identified. See *The Letters of Percy Bysshe Shelley*, ed. F. L. Jones (2 vols.; Oxford: Oxford University Press, 1964), II, 103.

awake, first suggested to me the conception of its fitness for a dramatic purpose. In fact it is a tragedy which has already received, from its capacity of awakening and sustaining the sympathy of men, approbation and success. Nothing remained, as I imagined, but to clothe it to the apprehensions of my countrymen in such language and action as would bring it home to their hearts. The deepest and the sublimest tragic compositions, King Lear, and the two plays in which the tale of Ædipus is told, were stories which already existed in tradition, as matters of popular belief and interest, before Shakespeare and Sophocles made them familiar to the sympathy of all succeeding generations of mankind.

This story of the Cenci is indeed eminently fearful and monstrous: anything like a dry exhibition of it on the stage would be insupportable. The person who would treat such a subject must increase the ideal, and diminish the actual horror of the events, so that the pleasure which arises from the poetry which exists in these tempestuous sufferings and crimes, may mitigate the pain of the contemplation of the moral deformity from which they spring. There must also be nothing attempted to make the exhibition subservient to what is vulgarly termed a moral purpose. The highest moral purpose aimed at in the highest species of the drama, is the teaching the human heart, through its sympathies and antipathies, the knowledge of itself; in proportion to the possession of which knowledge, every human being is wise, just, sincere, tolerant, and kind. If dogmas can do more, it is well: but a drama is no fit place for the enforcement of them. Undoubtedly no person can be truly dishonoured by the act of another; and the fit return to make to the most enormous injuries is kindness and forbearance, and a resolution to convert the injurer from his dark passions by peace and love. Revenge, retaliation, atonement, are pernicious mistakes. If Beatrice had thought in this manner she would have been wiser and better; but she would never have been a tragic character: the few whom such an exhibition would have interested, could never have been sufficiently interested for a dramatic purpose, from the want of finding sympathy in their interest among the mass who surround them. It is in the restless and anatomising casuistry with which men seek the justification of Beatrice, yet feel that she has done what needs justification; it is in the superstitious horror with which they contemplate alike her wrongs and their revenge, that the dramatic character of what she did and suffered, consists.

I have endeavoured as nearly as possible to represent the characters as they probably were, and have sought to avoid the error of making them actuated by my own conceptions of right or wrong, false or true: thus under a thin veil converting names and actions of the sixteenth century into cold impersonations of my own mind. They are represented as Catholics, and as Catholics deeply tinged with religion. To a Protestant apprehension there will appear something unnatural in the earnest and perpetual sentiment of the relations between God and man which pervade the tragedy of the Cenci. It will especially be startled at the combination of an undoubting persuasion of the truth of the popular religion with a cool and determined perseverance in enormous guilt. But religion in Italy is not, as in Protestant countries, a cloak to be worn on particular days; or a passport which those who do not wish to be railed at carry with them to exhibit; or a gloomy passion for penetrating the impenetrable mysteries of our being, which terrifies its possessor at the darkness of the abyss to the brink of which it has conducted him. Religion coexists, as it were, in the mind of an Italian Catholic, with a faith in that of which all men have the most certain knowledge. It is interwoven with the whole fabric of life. It is adoration, faith, submission, penitence, blind admiration; not a rule for moral conduct. It has no necessary connexion with any one virtue. The most atrocious villain may be rigidly devout, and, without any shock to established faith, confess himself to be so. Religion pervades intensely the whole frame of society, and is, according to the temper of the mind which it inhabits, a passion, a persuasion, an excuse, a refuge; never a check. Cenci himself built a chapel in the court of his palace, and dedicated it to St. Thomas the Apostle, and established masses for the peace of his soul. Thus in the first scene of the fourth act Lucretia's design in exposing herself to the consequences of an expostulation with Cenci after having administered the opiate, was to induce him by a feigned tale to confess himself before death; this being esteemed by Catholics as essential to salvation; and she only relinquishes her purpose when she perceives that her perseverance would expose Beatrice to new outrages.

I have avoided with great care in writing this play the introduction of what is commonly called mere poetry, and I imagine there will scarcely be found a detached simile or a single isolated description, unless Beatrice's description of the chasm appointed for her father's murder should be judged to be of that nature.[4]

In a dramatic composition the imagery and the passion should interpenetrate one another, the former being reserved simply for the full development and illustration of the latter. Imagination is as the immortal God which should assume flesh for the redemption of mortal passion. It is thus that the most remote and the most familiar imagery may alike be fit for dramatic purposes when employed in the illustration of strong feeling, which raises what is low, and levels to the apprehension that which is lofty, casting over all the shadow of its own greatness. In other respects I have written more carelessly; that is, without an over-fastidious and learned choice of words. In this respect, I entirely agree with those modern critics who assert that in order to move men to true sympathy we must use the familiar language of men. And that our great ancestors the ancient English poets are the writers, a study of whom might incite us to do that for our own age which they have done for theirs. But it must be the real language of men in general, and not that of any particular class to whose society the writer happens to belong. So much for what I have attempted; I need not be assured that success is a very different matter; particularly for one whose attention has but newly been awakened to the study of dramatic literature.

I endeavoured whilst at Rome to observe such monuments of this story as might be accessible to a stranger. The portrait of Beatrice at the Colonna Palace is admirable as a work of art: it was taken by Guido during her confinement in prison. But it is most interesting as a just representation of one of the loveliest specimens of the workmanship of Nature. There is a fixed and pale composure

4. An idea in this speech was suggested by a most sublime passage in *El Purgatorio de San Patricio* of Calderón, the only plagiarism which I have intentionally committed in the whole piece. [Shelley's note.]

upon the features: she seems sad and stricken down in spirit, yet the despair thus expressed is lightened by the patience of gentleness. Her head is bound with folds of white drapery, from which the yellow strings of her golden hair escape, and fall about her neck. The moulding of her face is exquisitely delicate; the eye-brows are distinct and arched; the lips have that permanent meaning of imagination and sensibility which suffering has not repressed and which it seems as if death scarcely could extinguish. Her forehead is large and clear; her eyes, which we are told were remarkable for their vivacity, are swollen with weeping and lustreless, but beautifully tender and serene. In the whole mien there is a simplicity and dignity which united with her exquisite loveliness and deep sorrow are inexpressibly pathetic. Beatrice Cenci appears to have been one of those rare persons in whom energy and gentleness dwell together without destroying one another: her nature was simple and profound. The crimes and miseries in which she was an actor and a sufferer are as the mask and the mantle in which circumstances clothed her for her impersonation on the scene of the world.

The Cenci Palace is of great extent; and, though in part modernized, there yet remains a vast and gloomy pile of feudal architecture in the same state as during the dreadful scenes which are the subject of this tragedy. The palace is situated in an obscure corner of Rome, near the quarter of the Jews, and from the upper windows you see the immense ruins of Mount Palatine half hidden under their profuse overgrowth of trees. There is a court in one part of the palace (perhaps that in which Cenci built the chapel to St. Thomas), supported by granite columns and adorned with antique friezes of fine workmanship, and built up according to the ancient Italian fashion, with balcony over balcony of open work. One of the gates of the palace, formed of immense stones, and leading through a passage dark and lofty, and opening into gloomy subterranean chambers, struck me particularly.

Of the Castle of Petrella, I could obtain no further information than that which is to be found in the manuscript.

The Complete Works of Percy Bysshe Shelley, ed. Roger Ingpen and Walter E. Peck (Julian Edition, 10 vols.; New York: Charles Scribner's Sons, 1926–1930), II, 67–74.

Preface to
Prometheus Unbound

Prometheus Unbound *was composed between September, 1818, and December, 1819; it was published in the summer of 1820. Thus the poem that many have called Shelley's masterpiece was interrupted by* The Cenci. *In the space of two years, few writers can have carried to completion two more diverse works. In each the aims are clearly defined. The preface to* Prometheus Unbound *first justifies the liberty Shelley has taken with the old story. His purpose is to exalt the character of Prometheus, "a more poetical character than Satan." The imagery of the play has been "drawn from the operations of the human mind, or from those external actions by which they are expressed"; this, Shelley asserts, is unusual in modern poetry. Poetry, he continues, "is a mimetic art. It creates, but it creates by combination and representation." Poets are thus the creators and the creations of their age. It is the recognition of this creative power that leads him to conclude, two years after* Laon *and* Cythna*: "Didactic poetry is my abhorrence; nothing can be equally well expressed in prose that is not supererogatory in verse." As in the preface to* The Cenci, *Shelley is concerned to preserve his own individuality and yet to acknowledge the relationship he felt to other poets of his time.*

[Do you not hear these things, Amphiaraus, hidden beneath the earth?][1]

The Greek tragic writers, in selecting as their subject any portion of their national history or mythology, employed in their treatment of it a certain arbitrary discretion. They by no means conceived themselves bound to adhere to the common interpretation or to

1. *"Audisne haec, amphiarae, sub terram abdite?"*

imitate in story as in title their rivals and predecessors. Such a system would have amounted to a resignation of those claims to preference over their competitors which incited the composition. The Agamemnonian story was exhibited on the Athenian theatre with as many variations as dramas.

I have presumed to employ a similar licence. The "Prometheus Unbound" of Æschylus supposed the reconciliation of Jupiter with his victim as the price of the disclosure of the danger threatened to his empire by the consummation of his marriage with Thetis. Thetis, according to this view of the subject, was given in marriage to Peleus, and Prometheus, by the permission of Jupiter, delivered from his captivity by Hercules. Had I framed my story on this model, I should have done no more than have attempted to restore the lost drama of Æschylus; an ambition, which, if my preference to this mode of treating the subject had incited me to cherish, the recollection of the high comparison such an attempt would challenge might well abate. But, in truth, I was averse from a catastrophe so feeble as that of reconciling the Champion with the Oppressor of mankind. The moral interest of the fable, which is so powerfully sustained by the sufferings and endurance of Prometheus, would be annihilated if we could conceive of him as unsaying his high language and quailing before his successful and perfidious adversary. The only imaginary being resembling in any degree Prometheus, is Satan; and Prometheus is, in my judgment, a more poetical character than Satan, because, in addition to courage, and majesty, and firm and patient opposition to omnipotent force, he is susceptible of being described as exempt from the taints of ambition, envy, revenge, and a desire for personal aggrandisement, which, in the Hero of Paradise Lost, interfere with the interest. The character of Satan engenders in the mind a pernicious casuistry which leads us to weigh his faults with his wrongs, and to excuse the former because the latter exceed all measure. In the minds of those who consider that magnificent fiction with a religious feeling it engenders something worse. But Prometheus is, as it were, the type of the highest perfection of moral and intellectual nature, impelled by the purest and the truest motives to the best and noblest ends.

This Poem was chiefly written upon the mountainous ruins of

the Baths of Caracalla, among the flowery glades, and thickets of odoriferous blossoming trees, which are extended in ever winding labyrinths upon its immense platforms and dizzy arches suspended in the air. The bright blue sky of Rome, and the effect of the vigorous awakening spring in that divinest climate, and the new life with which it drenches the spirits even to intoxication, were the inspiration of this drama.

The imagery which I have employed will be found, in many instances, to have been drawn from the operations of the human mind, or from those external actions by which they are expressed. This is unusual in modern poetry, although Dante and Shakespeare are full of instances of the same kind: Dante indeed more than any other poet, and with greater success. But the Greek poets, as writers to whom no resource of awakening the sympathy of their contemporaries was unknown, were in the habitual use of this power; and it is the study of their works, (since a higher merit would probably be denied me,) to which I am willing that my readers should impute this singularity.

One word is due in candour to the degree in which the study of contemporary writings may have tinged my composition, for such has been a topic of censure with regard to poems far more popular, and indeed more deservedly popular, than mine. It is impossible that any one who inhabits the same age with such writers as those who stand in the foremost ranks of our own, can conscientiously assure himself that his language and tone of thought may not have been modified by the study of the productions of those extraordinary intellects. It is true, that, not the spirit of their genius, but the forms in which it has manifested itself, are due less to the peculiarities of their own minds than to the peculiarity of the moral and intellectual condition of the minds among which they have been produced. Thus a number of writers possess the form, whilst they want the spirit of those whom, it is alleged, they imitate; because the former is the endowment of the age in which they live, and the latter must be the uncommunicated lightning of their own mind.

The peculiar style of intense and comprehensive imagery which distinguishes the modern literature of England, has not been, as a general power, the product of the imitation of any particular writer.

The mass of capabilities remains at every period materially the same; the circumstances which awaken it to action perpetually change. If England were divided into forty republics, each equal in population and extent to Athens, there is no reason to suppose but that, under institutions not more perfect than those of Athens, each would produce philosophers and poets equal to those who (if we except Shakespeare) have never been surpassed. We owe the great writers of the golden age of our literature to that fervid awakening of the public mind which shook to dust the oldest and most oppressive form of the Christian religion. We owe Milton to the progress and development of the same spirit: the sacred Milton was, let it ever be remembered, a republican, and a bold inquirer into morals and religion. The great writers of our own age are, we have reason to suppose, the companions and forerunners of some unimagined change in our social condition, or the opinions which cement it. The cloud of mind is discharging its collected lightning, and the equilibrium between institutions and opinions is now restoring, or is about to be restored.

As to imitation, poetry is a mimetic art. It creates, but it creates by combination and representation. Poetical abstractions are beautiful and new, not because the portions of which they are composed had no previous existence in the mind of man or in nature, but because the whole produced by their combination has some intelligible and beautiful analogy with those sources of emotion and thought, and with the contemporary condition of them: one great poet is a masterpiece of nature which another not only ought to study but must study. He might as wisely and as easily determine that his mind should no longer be the mirror of all that is lovely in the visible universe, as exclude from his contemplation the beautiful which exists in the writings of a great contemporary. The pretence of doing it would be a presumption in any but the greatest; the effect, even in him, would be strained, unnatural, and ineffectual. A poet is the combined product of such internal powers as modify the nature of others; and of such external influences as excite and sustain these powers; he is not one, but both. Every man's mind is, in this respect, modified by all the objects of nature and art; by every word and every suggestion which he ever admitted to act upon his consciousness; it is the mirror upon which all forms are reflected, and in which they compose one form. Poets, not otherwise than philosophers, painters, sculptors, and musicians, are, in one sense, the creators, and, in another, the creations, of their age. From this subjection the loftiest do not escape. There is a similarity between Homer and Hesiod, between Æschylus and Euripides, between Virgil and Horace, between Dante and Petrarch, between Shakespeare and Fletcher, between Dryden and Pope; each has a generic resemblance under which their specific distinctions are arranged. If this similarity be the result of imitation, I am willing to confess that I have imitated.

Let this opportunity be conceded to me of acknowledging that I have, what a Scotch philosopher characteristically terms, "a passion for reforming the world": what passion incited him to write and publish his book, he omits to explain. For my part, I had rather be damned with Plato and Lord Bacon, than go to Heaven with Paley and Malthus.[2] But it is a mistake to suppose that I dedicate my poetical compositions solely to the direct enforcement of reform, or that I consider them in any degree as containing a reasoned system on the theory of human life. Didactic poetry is my abhorrence; nothing can be equally well expressed in prose that is not tedious and supererogatory in verse. My purpose has hitherto been simply to familiarize the highly refined imagination of the more select classes of poetical readers with beautiful idealisms of moral excellence; aware that until the mind can love, and admire, and trust, and hope, and endure, reasoned principles of moral conduct are seeds cast upon the highway of life which the unconscious passenger tramples into dust, although they would bear the harvest of his happiness. Should I live to accomplish what I purpose, that is, produce a systematical history of what appear to me to be the genuine elements of human society, let not the advocates of injustice and superstition flatter themselves that I should take Æschlyus rather than Plato as my model.

The having spoken of myself with unaffected freedom will need little apology with the candid; and let the uncandid consider that

2. For identification of Paley and Malthus see Shelley's review of Godwin's *Mandeville*, p. 98, note 5.

they injure me less than their own hearts and minds by misrepresentation. Whatever talents a person may possess to amuse and
instruct others, be they ever so inconsiderable, he is yet bound to
exert them: if his attempt be ineffectual, let the punishment of an
unaccomplished purpose have been sufficient; let none trouble
themselves to heap the dust of oblivion upon his efforts; the pile
they raise will betray his grave which might otherwise have been
unknown.

The Complete Works of Percy Bysshe Shelley, ed. Roger Ingpen and Walter
E. Peck (Julian Edition, 10 vols.; New York: Charles Scribner's Sons,
1926–1930), II, 171–175.

Advertisement to *Oedipus Tyrannus*

Oedipus Tyrannus *was begun August 24, 1819, before Shelley had completed* Prometheus Unbound; *it was published anonymously in London the following year. Only seven copies were sold before the publisher surrendered the rest of the edition on threat of prosecution.*

This tragedy is one of a triad, or system of three Plays, (an arrangement according to which the Greeks were accustomed to connect their Dramatic representations,) elucidating the wonderful and appalling fortunes of the Swellfoot dynasty. It was evidently written by some *learned Theban*, and, from its characteristic dulness, apparently before the duties on the importation of *Attic salt* had been repealed by the Bœotarchs. The tenderness with which he beats the pigs proves him to have been a Bœotian swine [*sus Bœotiæ*]; possibly a glutton [*Epicuri de grege porcus*]; for, as the poet observes,

A fellow feeling makes us wond'rous kind.

No liberty has been taken with the translation of this remarkable piece of antiquity, except the suppressing a seditious and blasphemous Chorus of the Pigs and Bulls at the last act. The word Hoydipouse, (or more properly Œdipus,) has been rendered literally Swellfoot, without its having been conceived necessary to determine whether a swelling of the hind or the fore feet of the Swinish Monarch is particularly indicated.

Should the remaining portions of this Tragedy be found, entitled, "*Swellfoot in Angaria*," and "*Charite*," the Translator might be tempted to give them to the reading Public.

The Complete Works of Percy Bysshe Shelley, ed. Roger Ingpen and Walter E. Peck (Julian Edition, 10 vols.; New York: Charles Scribner's Sons, 1926–1930), II, 321.

Advertisement to *Epipsychidion*

Epipsychidion was composed in January and February, 1821; it was published anonymously in 1822. The title, a coinage by Shelley, is intended to mean "a soul within a soul" or "a soul upon a soul." In his letter to his publisher, Charles Ollier, February 16, 1821, Shelley speaks of the "Advertisement" as "no fiction," since his disillusion with Emilia Viviani was a kind of death.

EPIPSYCHIDION: Verses Addressed to the
Noble and Unfortunate Lady, Emilia V ——
Now Imprisoned in the Convent of ——

["The loving soul launches itself out from the world and makes itself a world in the infinite, all for itself very different from this dim and fearful abysm." [1]]

The writer of the following Lines died at Florence, as he was preparing for a voyage to one of the wildest of the Sporades, which he had bought, and where he had fitted up the ruins of an old building, and where it was his hope to have realised a scheme of life, suited perhaps to that happier and better world of which he is now an inhabitant, but hardly practicable in this. His life was singular; less on account of the romantic vicissitudes which diversified it, than the ideal tinge which it received from his own character and feelings. The present Poem, like the Vita Nuova of Dante, is sufficiently intelligible to a certain class of readers without a matter-of-fact history of the circumstances to which it relates; and to a certain other class it must ever remain incomprehensible, from a defect of a common organ of perception

1. "*L'anima amante si slancia fuori del creato, e si crea nell' infinito un Mondo tutto per essa, diverso assai da questo oscuro e pauroso baratro.*" Her own words. [Shelley's note.]

for the ideas of which it treats. Not but that, "great were his shame who should rhyme anything under a garb of metaphor or rhetorical colour, and then, being asked, should be incapable of stripping his words of this garb so that they might have a veritable meaning." [2]

The present poem appears to have been intended by the Writer as the dedication to some longer one. The stanza on the above page is almost a literal translation from Dante's famous Canzone

You who intelligent the Third Heaven move. [3]

The presumptuous application of the concluding lines to his own composition will raise a smile at the expense of my unfortunate friend: be it a smile not of contempt, but pity.

The Complete Works of Percy Bysshe Shelley, ed. Roger Ingpen and Walter E. Peck (Julian Edition, 10 vols.; New York: Charles Scribner's Sons, 1926–1930), II, 355.

2. "*gran vergogna sarebbe a colui, che rimasse cosa sotto veste di figura, o di colore rettorico: e domandato non sapesse denudare le sue parole da cotal veste, in guisa che avessero verace intendimento.*" The translation above is by William Michael Rossetti in his edition of *Shelley's Poetical Works* (London: Gibbings and Company Ltd., 1894), II, 450. His brother, Dante Gabriel Rossetti, had translated Dante's *Vita Nuova* in 1861, but William Michael assisted in preparing that work for publication; see *The Collected Works of Dante Gabriel Rossetti*, ed. William M. Rossetti (London: Ellis and Elvey, 1901), II, 517.

3. "*Voi, ch' intendendo, il terzo ciel movete*, &c." The translation above is the first line of Shelley's version of "The First Canzone of the Convito" (*The Complete Poetical Works of Percy Bysshe Shelley*, ed. Thomas Hutchinson [London: Oxford University Press, 1904], p. 718).

Preface to *Adonais*

Keats died in Rome, February 23, 1821. Adonais *was written the following June, and printed in Italy by July 13. In England it was sold, and reviewed in several periodicals, but was not formally published until 1829, except for a pirated version in the* Literary Chronicle and Weekly Review, *December 1, 1821. Letters of this period throw light on Shelley's relations with Keats, and on the conception of the poem. Shelley greatly exaggerated the effect of the* Quarterly Review *on Keats's health, perhaps through reports from a Reverend Robert Finch, who knew Keats's companion in Italy, Joseph Severn (see notes in* The Letters of Percy Bysshe Shelley, *ed. F. L. Jones [2 vols.; Oxford: Oxford University Press, 1964], II, 299–300). In the preface, Shelley speaks of his "known repugnance to the narrow principles of taste" exemplified in Keats's early poems, notably* Endymion, *though a letter to the editor of the* Quarterly Review *specifies lines in* Endymion *that Shelley admired.* Hyperion *Shelley thought "second to nothing that was ever produced by a writer of the same years." It is surprising, however, that neither in the preface nor in his letters does Shelley allude to such poems in Keats's 1820 volume as "Isabella," "The Eve of St. Agnes," "Lamia," and the great odes.* Adonais *is less a comment on Keats than on the neglected poet as a type who illustrates the world's callous cruelty.*

ADONAIS: An Elegy on the Death of John Keats
Author of Endymion, Hyperion, Etc.

"Thou wert the morning star among the living
Ere thy fair light had fled:—
Now, having died, thou art as Hesperus, giving
New splendour to the dead."

Plato[1]

1.

Ἀστήρ πρὶν μὲν ἔλαμπες ἐνι ζώοισιν ἐῶος.
Νῦν δὲ θανών, λαμπιες ἔαπερος ἐν φθίμενοις.

72

"Poison came, Bion, to thy mouth, thou didst know poison.
To such lips as thine did it come, and was not sweetened?
What mortal was so cruel that could mix poison for thee,
or who could give thee the venom that heard thy voice?
surely he had no music in his soul."

Moschus. Epitaph. Bion.[2]

It is my intention to subjoin to the London edition of this poem,
a criticism upon the claims of its lamented object to be classed
among the writers of the highest genius who have adorned our age.
My known repugnance to the narrow principles of taste on which
several of his earlier compositions were modelled, prove, at least
that I am impartial judge. I consider the fragment of Hyperion, as
second to nothing that was ever produced by a writer of the same
years.

John Keats died at Rome of a consumption, in his twenty-fourth
year, on the —— of ——— 1821, and was buried in the romantic
and lonely cemetery of the protestants in that city, under the pyramid which is the tomb of Cestius, and the massy walls and towers,
now mouldering and desolate, which formed the circuit of ancient
Rome. The cemetery is an open space among the ruins covered
in winter with violets and daisies. It might make one in love with
death, to think that one should be buried in so sweet a place.

The genius of the lamented person to whose memory I have dedicated these unworthy verses, was not less delicate and fragile than
it was beautiful; and where canker-worms abound, what wonder,
if its young flower was blighted in the bud? The savage criticism
on his Endymion, which appeared in the Quarterly Review,

The translation from Plato given above is Shelley's own: "To Stella," *The Complete Works of Percy Bysshe Shelley*, ed. Roger Ingpen and Walter E. Peck (Julian
Edition, 10 vols.; New York: Charles Scribner's Sons, 1926–1930), IV, 283.

2.

Φάρμακον ἦλθε, Βίων, ποτὶ σὸν στόμα, φάρμακον εἶδες·
Πῶς τευ τοῖς χείλεσσι ποτέδραμε, κοὐκ ἐγλυκάνθη;
Τίς δὲ βροτὸς τοσσοῦτον ἀνάμερος, ἢ κεράσαι τοι,
Ἢ δοῦναι λαλέοντι, τὸ φάρμακον; ἔκφυγεν ᾠδάν.

The translation given above is by Andrew Lang, *Theocritus, Bion and Moschus*
(London: Macmillan, 1924; first published 1880), p. 202.

produced the most violent effect on his susceptible mind; the agitation thus originated ended in the rupture of a blood-vessel in the lungs; a rapid consumption ensued, and the succeeding acknowledgments from more candid critics, of the true greatness of his powers, were ineffectual to heal the wound thus wantonly inflicted.[3]

It may be well said, that these wretched men know not what they do. They scatter their insults and their slanders without heed as to whether the poisoned shaft lights on a heart made callous by many blows, or one, like Keats's, composed of more penetrable stuff. One of their associates is, to my knowledge, a most base and unprincipled calumniator. As to "Endymion," was it a poem, whatever might be its defects, to be treated contemptuously by those who had celebrated with various degrees of complacency and panegyric, "Paris," and "Woman," and a "Syrian Tale," and Mrs. Lefanu, and Mr. Barret, and Mr. Howard Payne, and a long list of the illustrious obscure?[4] Are these the men, who in their venal good-nature, presumed to draw a parallel between the Rev. Mr. Milman and Lord Byron? What gnat did they strain at here, after having swallowed all those camels? Against what woman taken in adultery dares the foremost of these literary prostitutes to cast his opprobrious stone? Miserable man! you, one of the meanest, have wantonly defaced one of the noblest specimens of

3. Shelley probably means Robert Southey, whom he had accused of attacking him and his *Revolt of Islam* anonymously in the *Quarterly Review* in 1817. The review, later attributed to Henry Hart Milman, is now known to have been written by Sir John Taylor Coleridge. (*The Letters of Percy Bysshe Shelley*, ed. F. L. Jones [2 vols.; Oxford: Oxford University Press, 1964], II, 299–300.)

4. *Paris in 1815, a Poem* was reviewed in the *Quarterly Review* for April, 1817, but the author was not identified. *Woman*, a volume of verse by Eaton Stannard Barrett, was published in 1810, but it was noticed in the *Quarterly* for April, 1818. Mrs. Lefanu was possibly Alicia Lefanu (1753–1817) or Alicia Lefanu (fl. 1812–1826), kinswomen of Philip Le Fanu (see *DNB*) who published romances. John Howard Payne, the American actor and playwright, wrote *Brutus, or the Fall of Tarquin, an Historical Tragedy*; it was produced at Drury Lane, December 3, 1818, and criticized adversely (not favorably, as Shelley implies) by the *Quarterly* in April, 1820. Later Payne was an unsuccessful suitor of Shelley's widow; he is chiefly remembered as the author of "Home, Sweet Home." William Michael Rossetti, in his edition of *Adonais* (Oxford: Clarendon Press, 1891), quotes from these reviews, pp. 97–98.

the workmanship of God. Nor shall it be your excuse, that, murderer as you are, you have spoken daggers, but used none.

The circumstances of the closing scene of poor Keats's life were not made known to me until the Elegy was ready for the press. I am given to understand that the wound which his sensitive spirit had received from the criticism of Endymion was exasperated at the bitter sense of unrequited benefits; the poor fellow seems to have been hooted from the stage of life, no less by those on whom he had wasted the promise of his genius, than those on whom he had lavished his fortune and his care. He was accompanied to Rome, and attended in his last illness by Mr. Severn, a young artist of the highest promise, who, I have been informed, "almost risked his own life, and sacrificed every prospect, to unwearied attendance upon his dying friend." Had I known these circumstances before the completion of my poem, I should have been tempted to add my feeble tribute of applause to the more solid recompense which the virtuous man finds in the recollection of his own motives. Mr. Severn can dispense with a reward from "such stuff as dreams are made of." His conduct is a golden augury of the success of his future career—may the unextinguished Spirit of his illustrious friend animate the creations of his pencil, and plead against Oblivion for his name!

The Complete Works of Percy Bysshe Shelley, ed. Roger Ingpen and Walter E. Peck (Julian Edition, 10 vols.; New York: Charles Scribner's Sons, 1926–1930), II, 387–388.

Preface to *Hellas*

Hellas *was composed in the autumn of 1821, and published in London the following spring. In his preface Shelley is apologetic. The drama, "if drama it must be called," is a "mere improvise." The occasion of the play was important to Shelley, but despite some notable lyrics,* Hellas *is the least important of his plays.*

The poem of Hellas, written at the suggestion of the events of the moment, is a mere improvise, and derives its interest (should it be found to possess any) solely from the intense sympathy which the Author feels with the cause he would celebrate.

The subject, in its present state, is insusceptible of being treated otherwise than lyrically, and if I have called this poem a drama, from the circumstance of its being composed in dialogue, the licence is not greater than that which has been assumed by other poets who have called their productions epics, only because they have been divided into twelve or twenty-four books.

The Persæ of Æschylus afforded me the first model of my conception, although the decision of the glorious contest now waging in Greece being yet suspended forbids a catastrophe parallel to the return of Xerxes and the desolation of the Persians. I have, therefore, contented myself with exhibiting a series of lyric pictures, and with having wrought upon the curtain of futurity, which falls upon the unfinished scene, such figures of indistinct and visionary delineation as suggest the final triumph of the Greek cause as a portion of the cause of civilisation and social improvement.

The drama (if drama it must be called) is, however, so inartificial that I doubt whether, if recited on the Thespian waggon to an Athenian village at the Dionysiaca, it would have obtained the prize of the goat. I shall bear with equanimity any punishment greater than the loss of such a reward which the Aristarchi of the hour may think fit to inflict.

The only *goat-song* which I have yet attempted has, I confess, in spite of the unfavourable nature of the subject, received a greater and a more valuable portion of applause than I expected or than it deserved.

Common fame is the only authority which I can allege for the details which form the basis of the poem, and I must trespass upon the forgiveness of my readers for the display of newspaper erudition to which I have been reduced. Undoubtedly, until the conclusion of the war, it will be impossible to obtain an account of it sufficiently authentic for historical materials; but poets have their privilege, and it is unquestionable that actions of the most exalted courage have been performed by the Greeks—that they have gained more than one naval victory, and that their defeat in Wallachia was signalised by circumstances of heroism more glorious even than victory.

The apathy of the rulers of the civilised world, to the astonishing circumstance of the descendants of that nation to which they owe their civilisation—rising as it were from the ashes of their ruin, is something perfectly inexplicable to a mere spectator of the shows of this mortal scene. We are all Greeks. Our laws, our literature, our religion, our arts, have their root in Greece. But for Greece—Rome the instructor, the conqueror, or the metropolis of our ancestors, would have spread no illumination with her arms, and we might still have been savages and idolaters; or, what is worse, might have arrived at such a stagnant and miserable state of social institutions as China and Japan possess.

The human form and the human mind attained to a perfection in Greece which has impressed its image on those faultless productions, whose very fragments are the despair of modern art, and has propagated impulses which cannot cease, through a thousand channels of manifest or imperceptible operation, to ennoble and delight mankind until the extinction of the race.

The modern Greek is the descendant of those glorious beings whom the imagination almost refuses to figure to itself as belonging to our kind, and he inherits much of their sensibility, their rapidity of conception, their enthusiasm, and their courage. If in many instances he is degraded by moral and political slavery to the practice of the basest vices it engenders, and that below the level of ordinary degradation; let us reflect that the corruption of the best produces the worst, and that habits which subsist only in relation to a peculiar state of social institution may be expected to cease as soon as that relation is dissolved. In fact, the Greeks, since the admirable novel of "Anastatius" [1] could have been a faithful picture of their manners, have undergone most important changes; the flower of their youth returning to their country from the universities of Italy, Germany, and France, have communicated to their fellow-citizens the latest results of that social perfection of which their ancestors were the original source. The university of Chios contained before the breaking out of the revolution eight hundred students, and among them several Germans and Americans. The munificence and energy of many of the Greek princes and merchants, directed to the renovation of their country with a spirit and a wisdom which has few examples, is above all praise.

The English permit their own oppressors to act according to their natural sympathy with the Turkish tyrant, and to brand upon their name the indelible blot of an alliance with the enemies of domestic happiness, of Christianity and civilisation.

Russia desires to possess, not to liberate Greece; and is contented to see the Turks, its natural enemies, and the Greeks, its intended slaves, enfeeble each other, until one or both fall into its net. The wise and generous policy of England would have consisted in establishing the independence of Greece, and in maintaining it both against Russia and the Turk;—but when was the oppressor generous or just?

Should the English people ever become free, they will reflect upon the part which those who presume to represent their will have played in the great drama of the revival of liberty, with feelings which it would become them to anticipate. This is the age of the war of the oppressed against the oppressors, and everyone of those ringleaders of the privileged gangs of murderers and

1. *Anastasius, or Memoirs of a Greek Written at the Close of the Eighteenth Century* (1819), a novel by Thomas Hope (1770–1831).

swindlers, called Sovereigns, look to each other for aid against the common enemy, and suspend their mutual jealousies in the presence of a mightier fear. Of this holy alliance all the despots of the earth are virtually members. But a new race has arisen throughout Europe, nursed with abhorrence of the opinions which are its chains, and she will continue to produce fresh generations to accomplish that destiny which tyrants foresee and dread.

The Spanish Peninsula is already free. France is tranquil in the enjoyment of a partial exemption from the abuses which its unnatural and feeble government are vainly attempting to revive. The seed of blood and misery has been sown in Italy, and a more vigorous race is arising to go forth to the harvest. The world waits only the news of a revolution of Germany, to see the tyrants who have pinnacled themselves on its supineness precipitated into the ruin from which they shall never arise. Well do these destroyers of mankind know their enemy, when they impute the insurrection in Greece to the same spirit before which they tremble throughout the rest of Europe, and that enemy well knows the power and cunning of its opponents, and watches the moment of their approaching weakness and inevitable division to wrest the bloody sceptres from their grasp.

The Complete Works of Percy Bysshe Shelley, ed. Roger Ingpen and Walter E. Peck (Julian Edition, 10 vols.; New York: Charles Scribner's Sons, 1926–1930), III, 7–10.

Preface to *Julian and Maddalo*

Julian and Maddalo *was composed in the autumn of 1818, after Shelley's first visit to Byron in Venice. The poem was to have been published anonymously the following year, but it first appeared in* Posthumous Poems *(1824). In his letters, Shelley's numerous comments on Byron supplement his characterisation of Maddalo. Julian, of course, is Shelley himself.*

Count Maddalo is a Venetian nobleman of ancient family and of great fortune, who, without mixing much in the society of his countrymen, resides chiefly at his magnificent palace in that city. He is a person of the most consummate genius, and capable, if he would direct his energies to such an end, of becoming the redeemer of his degraded country. But it is his weakness to be proud: he derives, from a comparison of his own extraordinary mind with the dwarfish intellects that surround him, an intense apprehension of the nothingness of human life. His passions and his powers are incomparably greater than those of other men; and, instead of the latter having been employed in curbing the former, they have mutually lent each other strength. His ambition preys upon itself, for want of objects which it can consider worthy of exertion. I say that Maddalo is proud, because I can find no other word to express the concentered and impatient feelings which consume him; but it is on his own hopes and affections only that he seems to trample, for in social life no human being can be more gentle, patient, and unassuming than Maddalo. He is cheerful, frank, and witty. His more serious conversation is a sort of intoxication; men are held by it as by a spell. He has travelled much; and there is an inexpressible charm in his relation of his adventures in different countries.

Julian is an Englishman of good family, passionately attached to those philosophical notions which assert the power of man over his own mind, and the immense improvements of which, by the extinction of certain moral superstitions, human society may be yet susceptible. Without concealing the evil in the world, he is for ever speculating how good may be made superior. He is a complete infidel, and a scoffer at all things reputed holy; and Maddalo takes a wicked pleasure in drawing out his taunts against religion. What Maddalo thinks on these matters is not exactly known. Julian, in spite of his heterodox opinions, is conjectured by his friends to possess some good qualities. How far this is possible the pious reader will determine. Julian is rather serious.

Of the Maniac I can give no information. He seems, by his own account, to have been disappointed in love. He was evidently a very cultivated and amiable person when in his right senses. His story, told at length, might be like many other stories of the same kind: the unconnected exclamations of his agony will perhaps be found a sufficient comment for the text of every heart.

The Complete Works of Percy Bysshe Shelley, ed. Roger Ingpen and Walter E. Peck (Julian Edition, 10 vols.; New York: Charles Scribner's Sons, 1926–1930), III, 177–178.

Dedication to
Peter Bell the Third

Wordsworth's "Peter Bell," the story of a sinful man converted to virtue through the patient loyalty of a donkey, though composed in 1798, was not published until 1819. John Hamilton Reynolds published a parody entitled Peter Bell, A Lyrical Ballad *(reprinted in Forman's edition of Shelley [1880], III, 446–458); the original poem and the parody were reviewed by Leigh Hunt in the* Examiner. *Shelley's poem was composed in the period May to November, 1819, and sent to England for anonymous publication. It first appeared in the second edition of* Poetical Works *(1839). "Thomas Brown," to whom the poem is dedicated, is a complimentary reference to Thomas Moore, whose satirical verse narratives about the Fudge Family were very popular. Shelley implies that Moore rivals Thomas Brown, the famous seventeenth-century wit. "Miching Mallecho," Shelley's pseudonym, derives from Hamlet's speech to Ophelia, III.ii.146–147.*

DEDICATION
TO THOMAS BROWN, ESQ., THE YOUNGER, H.F.

Dear Tom,

Allow me to request you to introduce Mr. Peter Bell to the respectable family of the Fudges; although he may fall short of those very considerable personages in the more active properties which characterize the Rat and the Apostate, I suspect that even you, their historian, will confess that he surpasses them in the more peculiarly legitimate qualification of intolerable dulness.

You know Mr. Examiner Hunt; well—it was he who presented me to two of the Mr. Bells. My intimacy with the younger Mr. Bell naturally sprung from this introduction to his brothers. And in presenting him to you, I have the satisfaction of being able to assure you that he is considerably the dullest of the three.

There is this particular advantage in an acquaintance with any one of the Peter Bells, that if you know one Peter Bell, you know three Peter Bells; they are not one, but three; not three, but one. An awful mystery, which, after having caused torrents of blood, and having been hymned by groans enough to deafen the music of the spheres, is at length illustrated to the satisfaction of all parties in the theological world, by the nature of Mr. Peter Bell.

Peter is a polyhedric Peter, or a Peter with many sides. He changes colours like a cameleon, and his coat like a snake. He is a Proteus of a Peter. He was at first sublime, pathetic, impressive, profound; then dull; then prosy and dull; and now dull—O, so very dull! it is an ultra-legitimate dulness.

You will perceive that it is not necessary to consider Hell and the Devil as supernatural machinery. The whole scene of my epic is in "this world which is"—So Peter informed us before his conversion to *White Obi*—

> —The world of all of us, *and where*
> *We find our happiness, or not at all.*[1]

Let me observe that I have spent six or seven days in composing this sublime piece; the orb of my moon-like genius has made the fourth part of its revolution round the dull earth which you inhabit, driving you mad, while it has retained its calmness and its splendour,

1. Obi is a type of African witchcraft. In a short poem of 1816, "Verses on Receiving a Celandine in a Letter from England" (*The Complete Works of Percy Bysshe Shelley*, ed. Roger Ingpen and Walter E. Peck [Julian Edition, 10 vols.; New York: Charles Scribner's Sons, 1926–1930], III, 124–126), Shelley had lamented the political conservatism of Wordsworth, signalized by his "Ode: The Morning of the Day Appointed for a General Thanksgiving. January 18, 1816" (*The Poems of Wordsworth*, ed. Thomas Hutchinson [New York: Oxford University Press, 1933], pp. 329–332). The passage quoted from Wordsworth (with Shelley's italics) appears in *The Prelude*, XI, 143–144; it was included in *Poems* (1815) entitled "French Revolution, as it Appeared to Enthusiasts at its Commencement. Reprinted from *The Friend*."

and I have been fitting this its last phase "to occupy a permanent station in the literature of my country." [2]

Your works, indeed, dear Tom, sell better; but mine are far superior. The public is no judge; posterity sets all to rights.

Allow me to observe that so much has been written of Peter Bell, that the present history can be considered only, like the Iliad, as a continuation of that series of cyclic poems, which have already been candidates for bestowing immortality upon, at the same time that they receive it from, his character and adventures. In this point of view I have violated no rule of syntax in beginning my composition with a conjunction; the full stop which closes the poem continued by me, being like the full stops at the end of the Iliad and Odyssey, a full stop of a very qualified import.

Hoping that the immortality which you have given to the Fudges, you will receive from them; and in the firm expectation, that when London shall be an habitation of bitterns, when St. Paul's and Westminster Abbey shall stand, shapeless and nameless ruins, in the midst of an unpeopled marsh; when the piers of Waterloo-Bridge shall become the nuclei of islets of reeds and osiers, and cast the jagged shadows of their broken arches on the solitary stream, some transatlantic commentator will be weighing in the scales of some new and now unimagined system of criticism, the respective merits of the Bells and the Fudges, and their historians,

I remain, dear Tom,

Yours sincerely

MICHING MALLECHO.

December 1, 1819.

P.S.—Pray excuse the date of place; so soon as the profits of the publication come in, I mean to hire lodgings in a more respectable street.

The Complete Works of Percy Bysshe Shelley, ed. Roger Ingpen and Walter E. Peck (Julian Edition, 10 vols.; New York: Charles Scribner's Sons, 1926–1930), III, 255–256.

2. Wordsworth's preface to *Peter Bell* referred to his repeated revisions of the poem between 1798 and 1819 "to make the production less unworthy of a favourable reception; or rather to fit it for filling *permanently* a station, however humble, in the Literature of our Country." Shelley's omission of "however humble" was probably deliberate satire.

Preface to the Translation of Plato's
The Banquet

The translation and Shelley's comment on it were composed in 1818. They were first published by Mary Shelley in Essays, Letters from Abroad, Translations and Fragments *(1840). Shelley's translation of this Platonic dialogue has frequently been reprinted.*

ON THE SYMPOSIUM,
OR PREFACE TO THE BANQUET OF PLATO
A FRAGMENT

The dialogue entitled "The Banquet," was selected by the translator as the most beautiful and perfect among all the works of Plato.[1] He despairs of having communicated to the English language any portion of the surpassing graces of the composition, or having done more than present an imperfect shadow of the language and the sentiment of this astonishing production.

Plato is eminently the greatest among the Greek philosophers, and from, or, rather, perhaps through him, his master Socrates, have proceeded those emanations of moral and metaphysical knowledge, on which a long series and an incalculable variety of popular superstitions have sheltered their absurdities from the slow contempt of mankind. Plato exhibits the rare union of close and subtle logic, with the Pythian enthusiasm of poetry, melted by the

1. *The Republic*, though replete with considerable errors of speculation, is, indeed, the greatest repository of important truths of all the works of Plato. This, perhaps, is because it is the longest. He first, and perhaps last, maintained that a state ought to be governed, not by the wealthiest, or the most ambitious, or the most cunning, but by the wisest; the method of selecting such rulers, and the laws by which such a selection is made, must correspond with and arise out of the moral freedom and refinement of the people. [Shelley's note.]

splendour and harmony of his periods into one irresistible stream of musical impressions, which hurry the persuasions onward, as in a breathless career. His language is that of an immortal spirit, rather than a man. Lord Bacon is, perhaps, the only writer, who, in these particulars, can be compared with him: his imitator, Cicero, sinks in the comparison into an ape mocking the gestures of a man. His views into the nature of mind and existence are often obscure, only because they are profound; and though his theories respecting the government of the world, and the elementary laws of moral action, are not always correct, yet there is scarcely any of his treatises which do not, however stained by puerile sophisms, contain the most remarkable intuitions into all that can be the subject of the human mind. His excellence consists especially in intuition, and it is this faculty which raises him far above Aristotle, whose genius, though vivid and various, is obscure in comparison with that of Plato.

The dialogue entitled the "Banquet," is called Ερωτικος, or a Discussion upon Love, and is supposed to have taken place at the house of Agathon, at one of a series of festivals given by that poet, on the occasion of his gaining the prize of tragedy at the Diony-siaca. The account of the debate on this occasion is supposed to have been given by Apollodorus, a pupil of Socrates, many years after it had taken place, to a companion who was curious to hear it. This Apollodorus appears, both from the style in which he is repre-sented in this piece, as well as from a passage in the *Phædon*, to have been a person of an impassioned and enthusiastic disposition; to borrow an image from the Italian painters, he seems to have been the St. John of the Socratic group. The drama (for so the lively distinction of character and the various and well-wrought circum-stances of the story almost entitle it to be called) begins by Socrates persuading Aristodemus to sup at Agathon's, uninvited. The whole of this introduction affords the most lively conception of refined Athenian manners.

[Unfinished.]

The Complete Works of Percy Bysshe Shelley, ed. Roger Ingpen and Walter E. Peck (Julian Edition, 10 vols.; New York: Charles Scribner's Sons, 1926–1930), VII, 161–162.

REVIEWS

Review of Hogg's
Memoirs of Prince Alexy Haimatoff

The Memoirs of Prince Alexy Haimatoff *was written by Shelley's friend Thomas Jefferson Hogg and published as a "translation from the original Latin" under the pseudonym of John Brown in 1813. Shelley's review appeared in* The Critical Review, *December, 1814; it was identified by Edward Dowden through a passage in Mary Shelley's journal. Shelley had also praised the novel in a letter to Hogg, November 26, 1813. For a Folio Society reprint of the novel (London, 1952) Sidney Scott provided an introduction identifying Alexy as Hogg, Rosalie as Harriet Shelley, and Gothon as Dr. Lind of Eton. Shelley and Hogg had quarreled over Hogg's attempt to seduce Harriet in 1811, but were reconciled the following year. Though Shelley's review was motivated by friendship for Hogg, objections are made to the carelessness of construction in the novel and to its implied condonation of sexual promiscuity. The passages Shelley quotes as praiseworthy seem conventional examples of the romantic fiction of the time.*

Is the suffrage of mankind the legitimate criterion of intellectual energy? Are complaints of the aspirants to literary fame, to be considered as the honourable disappointment of neglected genius, or the sickly impatience of a dreamer miserably self-deceived? the most illustrious ornaments of the annals of the human race, have been stigmatised by the contempt and abhorrence of entire communities of man; but this injustice arose out of some temporary superstition, some partial interest, some national doctrine: a glorious redemption awaited their remembrance. There is indeed, nothing so remarkable in the contempt of the ignorant for the enlightened: the vulgar pride of folly, delights to triumph upon mind. This is an intelligible process: the infamy or ingloriousness that can be thus explained, detracts nothing from the beauty of virtue or the sublimity of genius. But what does utter obscurity express? if the public do not advert even in censure to a performance, has the performance already received its condemnation?

The result of this controversy is important to the ingenuous critic. His labours are indeed, miserably worthless, if their objects may invariably be attained before their application. He should know the limits of his prerogative. He should not be ignorant, whether it is his duty to promulgate the decisions of others, or to cultivate his taste and judgment that he may be enabled to render a reason for his own.

Circumstances the least connected with intellectual nature have contributed, for a certain period, to retain in obscurity, the most memorable specimens of human genius. The author refrains perhaps from introducing his production to the world with all the pomp of empirical bibliopolism. A sudden tide in the affairs of men may make the neglect or contradiction of some insignificant doctrine, a badge of obscurity and discredit: those even who are exempt from the action of these absurd predilections, are necessarily in an indirect manner affected by their influence. It is perhaps the product of an imagination daring and undisciplined: the majority of readers ignorant and disdaining toleration refuse to pardon a neglect of common rules; their canons of criticism are carelessly infringed, it is less religious than a charity sermon, less methodical and cold than a French tragedy, where all the unities are preserved: no excellencies, where prudish cant and dull regularity are absent, can preserve it from the contempt and abhorrence of the multitude. It is evidently not difficult to imagine an instance in which the most elevated genius shall be recompensed with neglect. Mediocrity alone seems unvaryingly to escape rebuke and obloquy, it accommodates its attempts to the spirit of the age, which has produced it, and adopts with mimic effrontery the cant of the day and hour for which alone it lives.

We think that "the Memoirs of Prince Alexy Haimatoff" deserves to be regarded as an example of the fact, by the frequency of which, criticism is vindicated from the imputation of futility and impertinence. We do not hesitate to consider this fiction, as the product of a bold and original mind. We hardly remember ever to have seen surpassed the subtle delicacy of imagination, by which the manifest distinctions of character, and form are seized and pictured in colours, that almost make nature more beautiful than herself. The vulgar observe no resemblances or discrepancies, but such as are gross and glaring. The science of mind to which history, poetry, biography serve as the materials, consists in the discernment of shades and distinctions where the unenlightened discover nothing but a shapeless and unmeaning mass. The faculty for this discernment distinguishes genius from dulness. There are passages in the production before us, which afford instances of just and rapid intuition belonging only to intelligences that possess this faculty in no ordinary degree. As a composition the book is far from faultless. Its abruptness and angularities do not appear to have received the slightest polish or correction. The author has written with fervour but has disdained to revise at leisure. These errors are the errors of youth and genius and the fervid impatience of sensibilities impetuously disburthening their fulness. The author is proudly negligent of connecting the incidents of his tale. It appears more like the recorded day dream of a poet, not unvisited by the sublimest and most lovely visions, than the tissue of a romance skilfully interwoven for the purpose of maintaining the interest of the reader, and conducting his sympathies by dramatic gradations to the denouement. It is, what it professes to be, a memoir, not a novel. Yet its claims to the former appellation are established, only by the impatience and inexperience of the author, who, possessing in an eminent degree, the higher qualifications of a novelist, we had almost said a poet, has neglected the number by which that success would probably have been secured, which, in this instance, merits of a far nobler stamp, have unfortunately failed to acquire. Prince Alexy is by no means an unnatural, although no common character. We think we can discern his counterpart in Alfieri's delineation of himself. The same propensities, the same ardent devotion to his purposes, the same chivalric and unproductive attachment to unbounded liberty, characterizes both. We are inclined to doubt whether the author has not attributed to his hero, the doctrines of universal philanthropy in a spirit of profound and almost unsearchable irony: at least he appears biassed by no peculiar principles, and it were perhaps an insoluble inquiry whether any, and if any, what moral truth he designed to illustrate by his tale. Bruhle, the tutor of Alexy, is a character delineated with consummate skill; the power of intelligence and virtue over external deficiencies, is forcibly exemplified. The calmness, patience and magnanimity of this singular man, are truly rare and admirable: his disinterestedness, his equanimity, his irresistible gentleness form a finished and delightful portrait. But we cannot regard his commendation to his pupil to indulge in promiscuous concubinage without horror and detestation. The author appears to deem the loveless intercourse of brutal appetite, a venial offence against delicacy and virtue! he asserts that a transient connection with a cultivated female, may contribute to form the heart without essentially vitiating the sensibilities. It is our duty to protest against so pernicious and disgusting an opinion. No man can rise pure from the poisonous embraces of a prostitute, or sinless from the desolated hopes of a confiding heart. Whatever may be the claims of chastity, whatever the advantages of simple and pure affections, these ties, these benefits are of equal obligation to either sex. Domestic relations depend for their integrity upon a complete reciprocity of duties. But the author himself has in the adventure of the sultana, Debesh-Sheptuti afforded a most impressive and tremendous allegory of the cold blooded and malignant selfishness of sensuality.

We are incapacitated by the unconnected and vague narrative from forming an analysis of the incidents; they would consist indeed, simply of a catalogue of events, and which, divested of the aërial tinge of genius might appear trivial and common. We shall content ourselves, therefore with selecting some passages calculated to exemplify the peculiar powers of the author. The following description of the simple and interesting Rosalie is in the highest style of delineation: "Her hair was unusually black, she truly had raven locks, the same glossiness, the same varying shade, the same mixture of purple and sable for which the plumage of the raven is remarkable, were found in the long elastic tresses depending from her head and covering her shoulders. Her complexion was dark and clear; the colours which composed the brown that dyed her smooth skin, were so well mixed, that not one blot, not one varied tinge injured its brightness, and when the blush of animation or of modesty flushed her cheek, the tint was so rare, that could a painter have dipped his pencil in it, that single shade would have rendered him immortal. The bone above her eye was sharp, and beautifully curved; much as I have admired the wonderful properties of curves, I am convinced that their most stupendous properties collected, would fall far short of that magic line. The eyebrow was pencilled with extreme nicety; in the centre it consisted of the deepest shade of black, at the edges it was hardly perceptible, and no man could have been hardy enough to have attempted to define the precise spot at which it ceased: in short the velvet drapery of the eyebrow was only to be rivalled by the purple of the long black eyelashes that terminated the ample curtain. Rosalie's eyes were large and full; they appeared at a distance uniformly dark, but upon close inspection the inumerable strokes of various hues of infinite fineness and endless variety drawn in concentric circles behind the pellucid chrystal, filled the mind with wonder and admiration, and could only be the work of infinite power directed by infinite wisdom."

Alexy's union with Aür-Ahebeh the Circassian slave is marked by circumstances of deep pathos, and the sweetest tenderness of sentiment. The description of his misery and madness at her death, deserves to be remarked as affording evidence of an imagination vast, profound and full of energy.

Alexy, who gained the friendship, perhaps the love of the native Rosalie: the handsome Haimatoff, the philosophic Haimatoff, the haughty Haimatoff, Haimatoff the gay, the witty, the accomplished, the bold hunter, the friend of liberty, the chivalric lover of all that is feminine, the hero, the enthusiast; see him now, that is he, mark him! he appears in the shades of evening, he stalks as a spectre, he has just risen from the damps of the charnel house; see, the dews still hang on his forehead. He will vanish at cock-crowing, he never heard the song of the lark, nor the busy hum of men; the sun's rays never warmed him, the pale moonbeam alone shews his unearthly figure, which is fanned by the wing of the owl, which scarce obstructs the slow flight of the droning beetle, or of the drowsy bat. Mark him! he stops, his lean arms are crossed on his bosom; he is bowed to the earth, his sunken eye gazes from its deep cavity on vacuity, as the toad skulking in the corner of a sepulchre, peeps with malignity through the circumambient gloom. His cheek is hollow; the glowing tints of his complexion, which once resembled the autumnal sunbeam on the autumnal beech, are gone, the cadaverous yellow, the livid hue have usurped their place, the sable honours of his head have perished, they once waved in the wind like the jetty pinions of the raven, the skull is only covered by the shrivelled skin, which the rook views wistfully, and calls to her young ones. His gaunt bones start from his wrinkled garments, his voice is deep, hollow, sepulchral; it is the voice which wakes the dead, he has long held converse with the departed. He attempts to walk he knows not whither, his legs totter under him, he falls, the boys hoot him, the dogs bark at him, he hears them not, he sees them not.—Rest there, Alexy, it beseemeth thee, thy bed is the grave, thy bride is the worm, yet once thou stoodest erect, thy cheek was flushed with joyful ardour, thy eye blazing told what thy head conceived, what thy heart felt, thy limbs were vigour and activity, thy bosom expanded with pride, ambition, and desire, every nerve thrilled to feel, every muscle swelled to execute.

Haimatoff, the blight has tainted thee, thou ample roomy web of life, whereon were traced the gaudy characters, the gay embroidery of pleasure, how has the moth battened on thee; Haimatoff, how has the devouring flame scorched the plains, once yellow with the harvest! the simoon, the parching breath of the desert, has swept over the laughing plains, the carpet of verdure rolled away at its approach, and has bared amid desolation. Thou stricken deer, thy leather coat, thy dappled hide hangs loose upon thee, it was a deadly arrow, how has it wasted thee, thou scathed oak, how has the red lightning drank thy sap: Haimatoff, Haimatoff, eat thy soul with vexation. Let the immeasurable ocean roll between thee and pride: you must not dwell together. (P. 129.)

The episode of Viola is affecting, natural, and beautiful. We do not ever remember to have seen the unforgiving fastidiousness of family honour more awfully illustrated. After the death of her lover, Viola still expects that he will esteem, still cherishes the delusion that he is not lost to her for ever.

She used frequently to go to the window to look for him, or walk in the Park to meet him, but without the least impatience, at his delay. She learnt a new tune, or a new song to amuse him, she stood behind the door to startle him as he entered, or disguised herself to surprise him.

The character of Mary, deserves, we think, to be considered as the only complete failure in the book. Every other female whom the author has attempted to describe is designated by an individuality peculiarly marked and true. They constitute finished portraits of whatever is eminently simple, graceful, gentle, or disgustingly atrocious and vile. Mary alone is the miserable parasite of fashion, the tame slave of drivelling and drunken folly, the cold hearted coquette, the lying and meretricious prude. The means employed to gain this worthless prize corresponds exactly with its worthlessness. Sir Fulke Hildebrand is a strenuous tory; Alexy, on his arrival in England professes himself inclined to the principles of the whig party, finding that the Baronet had sworn that his daughter should never marry a whig, he sacrifices his principles and with inconceiveable effrontery thus palliates his apostacy and falsehood.

> The prejudices of the Baronet, were strong in proportion as they were irrational. I resolved rather to humour than to thwart them. I contrived to be invited to dine in company with him; I always proposed the health of the minister, I introduced politics and defended the tory party in long speeches, I attended clubs and public dinners of that interest. I do not know whether this conduct was justifiable; it may certainly be excused when the circumstances of my case are duly considered. I would tear myself in pieces, if I suspected that I could be guilty of the slightest falsehood or prevarication; (see Lord Chesterfield's letters for the courtier-like distinction between simulation and dissimulation,) but there was nothing of that sort here. I was of no party, consequently, I could not be accused of deserting any one. I did not defend the injustice of any body of men, I did not detract from the merits of any virtuous character. I praised what was laudable in the tory party, and blamed what was reprehensible in the whigs: I was silent with regard to whatever was culpable in the former or praiseworthy in the latter. The stratagem was innocent, which injured no one, and which promoted the happiness of two individuals, especially of the most amiable woman the world ever knew.

An instance of more deplorable perversity of the human understanding we do not recollect ever to have witnessed. It almost persuades us to believe that scepticism or indifference concerning certain sacred truths may occasionally produce a subtlety of sophism, by which the conscience of the criminal may be bribed to overlook his crime.

Towards the conclusion of this strange and powerful performance it must be confessed that sometimes the good Homer nods.[1] The adventure of the Eleutheri, although the sketch of a profounder project, is introduced and concluded with unintelligible abruptness. Bruhle dies, purposely as it should seem that his pupil may renounce the romantic sublimity of his nature, and that his inauspicious union and prostituted character, might be exempt from the censure of violated friendship. Numerous indications of profound and vigorous thought are scattered over even the most negligently compacted portions of the narrative. It is an unweeded garden where nightshade is interwoven with sweet jessamine, and the most delicate spices of the east, peep over struggling stalks of rank and poisonous hemlock.

In the delineation of the more evanescent feelings and uncommon instances of strong and delicate passion we conceive the author to have exhibited new and unparalleled powers. He has noticed some peculiarities of female character, with a delicacy and truth singularly exquisite. We think that the interesting subject of sexual relations requires for its successful development the application of a mind thus organised and endowed. Yet even here how great the deficiencies; this mind must be pure from the fashionable superstitions of gallantry, must be exempt from the sordid feelings which with blind idolatry worship the image and blaspheme the deity, reverence the type, and degrade the reality of which it is an emblem.

We do not hesitate to assert that the author of this volume is a man of ability. His great though indisciplinable energies and fervid rapidity of conception embody scenes and situations, and passions affording inexhaustible food for wonder and delight. The interest is deep and irresistible. A moral enchanter seems to have conjured up the shapes of all that is beautiful and strange to suspend the faculties in fascination and astonishment.

The Complete Works of Percy Bysshe Shelley, ed. Roger Ingpen and Walter E. Peck (Julian Edition, 10 vols.; New York: Charles Scribner's Sons, 1926–1930), VI, 175–184.

1. "*aliquando bonus dormitat Homerus.*"

Review of Godwin's *Mandeville*

Mandeville was published in 1817; Shelley's review appeared in Leigh Hunt's Examiner, *December 28, as a letter to the editor. Godwin was then sixty-one, known for his novels, several of which Shelley mentions, and also for his* Enquiry Concerning Political Justice *(1793). This work of revolutionary philosophy Shelley had encountered about 1810, and early in 1812 he began a correspondence with Godwin. The two met later that year, and through the friendship Shelley met Godwin's daughter Mary, with whom he eloped in August, 1814. Godwin was indignant about the elopement, yet he continued to make heavy demands on Shelley for financial assistance. On the death of Harriet, Shelley's first wife, Shelley and Mary were formally married, December 30, 1816. The review of* Mandeville *shows no trace of these personal relationships.*

SIR,—The author of "Mandeville" is one of the most illustrious examples of intellectual power of the present age. He has exhibited that variety and universality of talent which distinguishes him who is destined to inherit lasting renown, from the possessors of temporary celebrity. If his claims were to be measured solely by the comprehension and accuracy of his researches into ethical and political science, still it would be difficult to name a contemporary competitor. Let us make a deduction of all those parts of his moral system which are liable to any possible controversy, and consider simply those which only to allege is to establish, and which belong to that most important class of truths, which he that announces to mankind seems less to teach than to recall.

"Political Justice"[1] is the first moral system explicitly founded upon the doctrine of the negativeness of rights and the positiveness

1. *An Enquiry Concerning Political Justice and Its Influence on General Virtue and Happiness* (1793).

of duties,—an obscure feeling of which has been the basis of all the
political liberty and private virtue in the world. But he is also the
author of "Caleb Williams";[2] and if we had no other record of a
mind but simply some fragment containing the conception of the
character of Falkland, doubtless we should say, "This is an extraordinary mind, and undoubtedly was capable of the very sublimest
enterprises of thought."

"St. Leon" and "Fleetwood"[3] are moulded, with somewhat
inferior distinctness, in the same character of an union of delicacy
and power. The "Essay on Sepulchres"[4] has all the solemnity and
depth of passion which belong to a mind that sympathizes, as one
man with his friend, in the interests of future ages, and in the
concerns of the vanished generations of mankind.

It may be said with truth, that Godwin has been treated unjustly
by those of his countrymen, upon whose favour temporary distinction depends. If he had devoted his high accomplishments to
flatter the selfishness of the rich, or enforced those doctrines on
which the powerful depend for power, they would no doubt
have rewarded him with their countenance, and he might have
been more fortunate in that sunshine than Mr. Malthus or Dr.
Paley.[5] But the difference would still have been as wide as that which
must for ever divide notoriety from fame. Godwin has been to
the present age in moral philosophy what Wordsworth is in poetry.
The personal interest of the latter would probably have suffered
from his pursuit of the true principles of taste in poetry, as much
as all that is temporary in the fame of Godwin has suffered from
his daring to announce the true foundation of morals, if servility,
and dependence, and superstition, had not been too easily recon-
cileable with Wordsworth's species of dissent from the opinions of

2. *Caleb Williams* (1794), Godwin's best-known novel, a fictional illustration of
the theories in his *Political Justice*.

3. *St. Leon* (1799) and *Fleetwood* (1805) were novels by Godwin.

4. *Essay on Sepulchres* (1809), a poem.

5. Thomas Robert Malthus (1766–1834), author of *An Essay on Population*,
published anonymously in 1798. Godwin published attacks on Malthus in 1801
and 1820. William Paley (1743–1805), Archdeacon of Carlisle, and author of
A View of the Evidences of Christianity (1794). Paley's *Evidences* was for three generations a standard defense of orthodox theology.

the great and the prevailing. It is singular, that the other nations of Europe should have anticipated in this respect the judgment of posterity, and that the name of Godwin, and that of his late illustrious and admirable wife, should be pronounced, even by those who know but little of English literature, with reverence: and that the writings of Mary Wollstonecraft should have been translated and universally read in France and Germany, long after the bigotry of faction has stifled them in our own country.

"Mandeville" is Godwin's last production. The interest of this novel is undoubtedly equal, in some respects superior, to that of "Caleb Williams." Yet there is no character like Falkland, whom the author, with that sublime casuistry which is the parent of toleration and forbearance, persuades us personally to love, whilst his actions must for ever remain the theme of our astonishment and abhorrence. Mandeville challenges our compassion, and no more. His errors arise from an immutable necessity of internal nature, and from much of a constitutional antipathy and suspicion, which soon sprang up into a hatred and contempt and barren misanthropy, which, as it had no root in genius or in virtue, produces no fruit uncongenial with the soil wherein it grew. Those of Falkland arose from a high, though perverted conception of the majesty of human nature, from a powerful sympathy with his species, and from a temper which led him to believe that the very reputation of excellence should walk among mankind, unquestioned and undefiled. So far as it was a defect to link the interest of the tale with any thing inferior to Falkland, so is "Mandeville" defective. But if the varieties of human character, the depth and complexity of human motive, those sources of the union of strength and weakness, those useful occasions for pleading in favour of universal kindness and toleration, are just subjects for illustration and developement in a work of fiction. "Mandeville" yields in interest and importance to none of the productions of the Author.

The language is more rich and various, and the expressions more eloquently sweet, without losing that energy and distinctness which characterizes "Political Justice" and "Caleb Williams." The moral speculations have a strength and consistency and boldness which has been less clearly aimed at in his other works of fiction.

The pleadings of Henrietta to Mandeville, after his recovery from madness, in favour of virtue and benevolent energy, compose, in every respect, the most perfect and beautiful piece of writing of modern times. It is the genuine doctrine of "Political Justice" presented in one perspicuous and impressive view, and clothed in such enchanting melody of language, as seems, scarcely less than the writings of Plato, to realize those lines of Milton:—

> How charming is divine Philosophy!
> Not harsh and crabbed, as dull fools suppose,
> But musical as is Apollo's lute.[6]

Clifford's talk, too, about wealth, has a beautiful and readily to be disentangled intermixture of truth and error. Clifford is a person, who, without those characteristics which usually constitute the sublime, is sublime from the mere excess of loveliness and innocence. Henrietta's first appearance to Mandeville at Mandeville House is an occurrence resplendent with the sunrise of life; it recalls to the memory many a vision,—or perhaps but one,—which the delusive exhalations of unbaffled hope has invested with a rose-like lustre as of morning, yet, unlike morning, a light, which, once extinguished, never can return. Henrietta seems at first to be all that a susceptible heart imagines in the object of its earliest passion. We scarcely can see her, she is so beautiful. There is a mist of dazzling loveliness which encircles her, and shuts out from the sight all that is mortal in her transcendent charms. But the veil is gradually withdrawn, and she "fades into the light of common day." [7] Her actions and even her sentiments do not correspond with the elevation of her speculative opinions, and the fearless purity which should be and is the accompaniment of truth and virtue. But she has a divided affection, and she is faithful there only where infidelity would have been self-sacrifice. Could the spotless Henrietta have subjected her love for Clifford to the vain and insulting accidents of wealth and reputation, and the babbling of a miserable old woman, and have proceeded unshrinkingly to her

6. Milton's *Comus*, ll. 476–478.
7. Wordsworth, "Ode on Intimations of Immortality," l. 76.

nuptial feast from the expostulations of Mandeville's impassioned and pathetic madness? It might be well in the Author to shew the foundations of human hope thus overturned, for his picture would otherwise have been illumined with one gleam of light; it was his skill to enforce the moral, "that all things are vanity," and that "the house of mourning is better than the house of feasting";[8] and we are indebted to those who make us feel the instability of our nature, that we may lay the knowledge which is its foundation deep, and make the affections which are its cement strong. But one regrets that Henrietta, who soared far beyond her contemporaries in her opinions, who was so beautiful, that she seemed a spirit among mankind, should act and feel no otherwise than the least exalted of her sex; and still more, that the Author capable of conceiving something so admirable and lovely, should have been withheld, by the tenour of the fiction which he chose, from executing it to its full extent. It almost seems in the original conception of the character of Henrietta, that something was imagined too vast and too uncommon to be realized; and the feeling weighs like disappointment on the mind.

But these, considered with reference to the core of the story, are extrinsical. The events of the tale flow on like the stream of fate, regular and irresistible, and growing at once darker and swifter in their progress;—there is no surprise, there is no shock: we are prepared for the worst from the very opening of the scene, though we wonder whence the author drew the shadows which render the moral darkness every instant more profound, and, at last, so appalling and complete. The interest is awfully deep and rapid. To struggle with it would be gossamer attempting to bear up against the tempest. In this respect it is more powerful than "Caleb Williams": the interest of "Caleb Williams" being as rapid but not so profound as that of "Mandeville." It is a wind which tears up the deepest waters of the ocean of mind. The reader's mind is hurried on, as he approaches the end, with breathless and accelerated impulse. The noun *Smorfia*[9] comes at last, and touches some nerve,

8. *Ecclesiastes* 7:2. The King James version reads: "It is better to go to the house of mourning, than to go to the house of feasting."

9. *Smorfia:* Italian for grimace.

which jars the inmost soul, and grates as it were along the blood; and we can scarcely believe that the grin, which must accompany Mandeville to his grave, is not stamped upon our own visage.

E. K.[10]

The Complete Works of Percy Bysshe Shelley, ed. Roger Ingpen and Walter E. Peck (Julian Edition, 10 vols.; New York: Charles Scribner's Sons, 1926–1930), VI, 219–223.

10. E. K. is an abbreviation of Mary's pet name for Shelley: Elfin Knight.

Preface to Mary Shelley's
Frankenstein; or, The Modern Prometheus

Frankenstein; or, the Modern Prometheus resulted from a friendly contest in producing ghost stories, engaged in by Shelley, his wife Mary, Byron, and Byron's physician, Dr. John Polidori, in Switzerland in 1816. Dr. Polidori published his novel, The Vampyre, *in April, 1819, attributing it to Byron. Byron then published his own brief fragment, with the same title, in the volume* Mazeppa *(1819).*[1] *Shelley did not complete a story, but he took great interest in Mary's narrative.* Frankenstein *was published in 1818; and according to Mary's statement in a later edition (1831), Shelley himself wrote the preface, in the assumed tone of the author herself. The significant critical perception is that the "impossible fact" on which the story is based afforded "a point of view to the imagination."*

The event on which this fiction is founded has been supposed, by Dr. Darwin[2] and some of the physiological writers of Germany, as not of impossible occurrence. I shall not be supposed as according the remotest degree of serious faith to such an imagination; yet, as in assuming it as a basis of a work of fancy, I have not considered myself as merely weaving a series of supernatural terrors. The event on which the interest of the story depends is exempt from the disadvantages of a mere tale of spectres or enchantment. It was recommended by the novelty of the situations which it develops: and, however impossible as a physical fact, affords a point of view to the imagination for the delineating of human passions more

1. See E. F. Bleiler, *Three Gothic Novels* (New York: Dover Publications, 1966).
2. Dr. Erasmus Darwin (1731–1802), author of botanical poems such as *The Loves of the Plants* (1789).

comprehensive and commanding than any which the ordinary relations of interesting events can yield.

I have thus endeavoured to preserve the truth of the elementary principles of human nature, while I have not scrupled to innovate upon their combinations. The *Iliad*, the tragic poetry of Greece,—Shakespeare, in the *Tempest* and *Midsummer Night's Dream*,—and most especially Milton, in *Paradise Lost*, conform to this rule; and the most humble novelist, who seeks to confer or receive amusement from his labours, may, without presumption, apply to prose fiction a licence, or rather a rule, from the adoption of which so many exquisite combinations of human feeling have resulted in the highest specimens of poetry.

The circumstance on which my story rests was suggested in casual conversation. It was commenced, partly as a source of amusement, and partly as an expedient for exercising any untried resources of mind. Other motives were mingled with these, as the work proceeded. I am by no means indifferent to the manner in which whatever moral tendencies exist in the sentiments or characters it contains shall affect the reader; yet my chief concern in this respect has been limited to the avoiding the enervating effects of the novels of the present day, and to the exhibition of the amiableness of domestic affection, and the excellence of universal virtue. The opinions which naturally spring from the character and situation of the hero are by no means to be conceived as existing always in my own conviction; nor is any inference justly to be drawn from the following pages as prejudicing any philosophical doctrine of whatever kind.

It is a subject also of additional interest to the author, that this story was begun in the majestic region where the scene is principally laid, and in society which cannot cease to be regretted. I passed the summer of 1816 in the environs of Geneva. The season was cold and rainy, and in the evenings we crowded around a blazing wood fire, and occasionally amused ourselves with some German stories of ghosts, which happened to fall into our hands. These tales excited in us a playful desire of imitation. Two other friends (a tale from the pen of one of whom would be far more acceptable to the public than any thing I can ever hope to produce) and myself agreed to write each a story, founded on some supernatural occurrence.

The weather, however, suddenly became serene; and my two friends left me on a journey among the Alps, and lost, in the magnificent scenes which they present, all memory of their ghostly visions. The following tale is the only one which has been completed.

The Complete Works of Percy Bysshe Shelley, ed. Roger Ingpen and Walter E. Peck (Julian Edition, 10 vols.; New York: Charles Scribner's Sons, 1926–1930), VI, 259–260.

Review of *Frankenstein*

This review was first published by Shelley's friend Thomas Medwin in the Athenaeum *for November 10, 1832; it was later included in the* Shelley Papers *(1833) and in subsequent collections of Shelley's prose.*

The novel of "Frankenstein; or, The Modern Prometheus," is undoubtedly, as a mere story, one of the most original and complete productions of the day. We debate with ourselves in wonder, as we read it, what could have been the series of thoughts—what could have been the peculiar experiences that awakened them— which conduced, in the author's mind, to the astonishing combinations of motives and incidents, and the startling catastrophe, which compose this tale. There are, perhaps, some points of subordinate importance, which prove that it is the author's first attempt. But in this judgment, which requires a very nice discrimination, we may be mistaken; for it is conducted throughout with a firm and steady hand. The interest gradually accumulates and advances towards the conclusion with the accelerated rapidity of a rock rolled down a mountain. We are led breathless with suspense and sympathy, and the heaping up of incident on incident, and the working of passion out of passion. We cry "hold, hold! enough!"—but there is yet something to come; and, like the victim whose history it relates, we think we can bear no more, and yet more is to be borne. Pelion is heaped on Ossa, and Ossa on Olympus. We climb Alp after Alp, until the horizon is seen blank, vacant, and limitless; and the head turns giddy, and the ground seems to fail under our feet.

This novel rests its claim on being a source of powerful and profound emotion. The elementary feelings of the human mind are exposed to view; and those who are accustomed to reason deeply on their origin and tendency will, perhaps, be the only persons who can sympathize, to the full extent, in the interest of the actions which are their result. But, founded on nature as they are, there is perhaps no reader, who can endure anything beside a new love-story, who will not feel a responsive string touched in his inmost soul. The sentiments are so affectionate and so innocent—the characters of the subordinate agents in this strange drama are clothed in the light of such a mild and gentle mind—the pictures of domestic manners are of the most simple and attaching character: the pathos is irresistible and deep. Nor are the crimes and male-volence of the single Being, though indeed withering and tre-mendous, the offspring of any unaccountable propensity to evil, but flow irresistibly from certain causes fully adequate to their production. They are the children, as it were, of Necessity and Human Nature. In this the direct moral of the book consists; and it is perhaps the most important, and of the most universal applica-tion, of any moral that can be enforced by example. Treat a person ill, and he will become wicked. Requite affection with scorn;—let one being be selected, for whatever cause, as the refuse of his kind—divide him, a social being, from society, and you impose upon him the irresistible obligations—malevolence and selfishness. It is thus that, too often in society, those who are best qualified to be its benefactors and its ornaments are branded by some accident with scorn, and changed, by neglect and solitude of heart, into a scourge and a curse.

The Being in "Frankenstein" is, no doubt, a tremendous creature. It was impossible that he should not have received among men that treatment which led to the consequences of his being a social nature. He was an abortion and an anomaly; and though his mind was such as its first impressions framed it, affectionate and full of moral sensibility, yet the circumstances of his existence are so monstrous and uncommon, that, when the consequences of them became developed in action, his original goodness was gradually turned into inextinguishable misanthropy and revenge. The scene between the Being and the blind De Lacey in the cottage is one of the most profound and extraordinary instances of pathos that we ever recollect. It is impossible to read this dialogue,—and indeed many others of a somewhat similar character,—without feeling the heart suspend its pulsations with wonder, and the "tears stream down the cheeks." The encounter and argument between Franken-stein and the Being on the sea of ice, almost approaches, in effect, to the expostulation of Caleb Williams with Falkland. It reminds us, indeed, somewhat of the style and character of that admirable writer, to whom the author has dedicated his work, and whose productions he seems to have studied.[1]

There is only one instance, however, in which we detect the least approach to imitation; and that is the conduct of the incident of Frankenstein's landing in Ireland. The general character of the tale, indeed, resembles nothing that ever preceded it. After the death of Elizabeth, the story, like a stream which grows at once more rapid and profound as it proceeds, assumes an irresistible solemnity, and the magnificent energy and swiftness of a tempest.

The churchyard scene, in which Frankenstein visits the tombs of his family, his quitting Geneva, and his journey through Tartary to the shores of the Frozen Ocean, resemble at once the terrible reanimation of a corpse and the supernatural career of a spirit. The scene in the cabin of Walton's ship—the more than mortal enthusiasm and grandeur of the Being's speech over the dead body of his victim—is an exhibition of intellectual and imaginative power, which we think the reader will acknowledge has seldom been surpassed.

The Complete Works of Percy Bysshe Shelley, ed. Roger Ingpen and Walter E. Peck (Julian Edition, 10 vols.; New York: Charles Scribner's Sons, 1926–1930), VI, 263–265.

1. *Frankenstein* was dedicated to Mary Shelley's father, William Godwin, himself a successful novelist. Caleb Williams and Falkland are characters in *Caleb Williams* (1794).

Review of Peacock's
Rhododaphne; or, The Thessalian Spell

The review of Thomas Love Peacock's Rhododaphne *was written in 1818, but was first published in 1879 when H. Buxton Forman found it among the Shelley papers; he included it in the Library Edition of Shelley's* Works *(1880). On November 28, 1817, Shelley had written favorably about the poem to Hogg. For a brief summary of Shelley's friendship with Peacock, see the headnote to Appendix B, "The Four Ages of Poetry," pp. 158–172.*

Rhododaphne is a poem of the most remarkable character, and the nature of the subject no less than the spirit in which it is written forbid us to range it under any of the classes of modern literature. It is a Greek and Pagan poem. In sentiment and scenery it is essentially antique. There is a strong religion of place [*religio loci*] throughout which almost compels us to believe that the author wrote from the dictation of a voice heard from some Pythian cavern in the solitudes where Delphi stood. We are transported to the banks of the Peneus and linger under the crags of Tempe, and see the water lilies floating on the stream. We sit with Plato by old Ilissus under the sacred Plane tree among the sweet scent of flowering sallows; and above there is the nightingale of Sophocles in the ivy of the pine, who is watching the sunset so that it may dare to sing; it is the radiant evening of a burning day, and the smooth hollow whirlpools of the river are overflowing with the aërial gold of the level sunlight. We stand in the marble temples of the Gods, and see their sculptured forms gazing and almost breathing around. We are led forth from the frequent pomp of sacrifice into the solitude of mountains and forests where Pan, "the life, the intellectual soul of grove and stream," yet lives and yet is worshipped. We visit the solitudes of Thessalian magic, and tremble with new wonder to hear statues speak and move and to see the shaggy changelings minister to their witch queen with the shape of beasts and the reason of men, and move among the animated statues who people her enchanted palaces and gardens. That wonderful overflowing of fancy the *Syria Dea* of Lucian, and the impassioned and elegant pantomime of Apuleius, have contributed to this portion of the poem. There is here, as in the songs of ancient times, music and dancing and the luxury of voluptuous delight. The Bacchanalians toss on high their leaf-inwoven hair, and the tumult and fervour of the chase is depicted; we hear its clamour gathering among the woods, and she who impels it is so graceful and so fearless that we are charmed—and it needs no feeble spell to see nothing of the agony and blood of that royal sport. This it is to be a scholar; this it is to have read Homer and Sophocles and Plato.

Such is the scenery and the spirit of the tale. The story itself presents a more modern aspect, being made up of combinations of human passion which seem to have been developed since the Pagan system has been outworn. The poem opens in a strain of elegant but less powerful versification than that which follows. It is descriptive of the annual festival of Love at his temple in Thespia. Anthemion is among the crowd of votaries; a youth from the banks of Arcadian Ladon:

> The flower of all Arcadia's youth
> Was he: such form and face, in truth,
> As thoughts of gentlest maidens seek
> In their day-dreams: soft glossy hair
> Shadowed his forehead, snowy-fair,
> With many a hyacinthine cluster:
> Lips, that in silence seemed to speak,
> Were his, and eyes of mild blue lustre:
> And even the paleness of his cheek,
> The passing trace of tender care,
> Still shewed how beautiful it were
> If its own natural bloom were there.—CANTO I, p. 11.

He comes to offer his vows at the shrine for the recovery of his mistress Calliroë, who is suffering under some strange, and as we are led to infer, magical disease. As he presents his wreath of flowers at the altar they are suddenly withered up. He looks and there is standing near him a woman of exquisite beauty who gives him another wreath which he places on the altar and it does not wither. She turns to him and bids him wear a flower which she presents, saying, with other sweet words—

> Some meet for once and part for aye,
> Like thee and me, and scarce a day
> Shall each by each remembered be:
> But take the flower I give to thee,
> And till it fades remember me.—CANTO I, p. 22.

As Anthemion passes from the temple among the sports and dances of the festival "with vacant eye"

> —the trains
> Of youthful dancers round him float,
> As the musing bard from his sylvan seat
> Looks on the dance of the noontide heat,
> Or the play of the watery flowers, that quiver
> In the eddies of a lowland river.—CANTO II, p. 29.

He there meets an old man who tells him that the flower he wears is the profane laurel-rose which grows in Larissa's unholy gardens, that it is impious to wear it in the temple of Love, and that he, who has suffered evils which he dares not tell from Thessalian enchantments, knows that the gift of this flower is a spell only to be dissolved by invoking his natal genius and casting the flower into some stream with the caution of not looking upon it after he has thrown it away. Anthemion obeys his direction, but so soon as he has . . .

.   .   .   .   .   .

> —round his neck
> Are closely twined the silken rings
> Of Rhododaphne's glittering hair,
> And round him her bright arms she flings,
> And cinctured thus in loveliest bands

> The charmèd waves in safety bear
> The youth and the enchantress fair
> And leave them on the golden sands.—CANTO V, pp. 110–11.

They now find themselves on a lonely moor on which stands a solitary cottage—ruined and waste; this scene is transformed by Thessalian magic to a palace surrounded by magnificent gardens. Anthemion enters the hall of the palace where, surrounded by sculptures of divine workmanship, he sees the earthly image of Uranian Love.

Plato says, with profound allegory, that Love is not itself beautiful, but seeks the possession of beauty; this idea seems embodied in the deformed dwarf who bids, with a voice as from a trumpet, Anthemion enter. After feast and music the natural result of the situation of the lovers is related by the poet to have place.

The last Canto relates the enjoyments and occupations of the lovers; and we are astonished to discover that any thing can be added to the gardens of Armida and Alcina, and the Bower of Bliss: the following description among many of a Bacchanalian dance is a remarkable instance of a fertile and elegant imagination.

> Oft, 'mid those palace-gardens fair,
> The beauteous nymph (her radiant hair
> With mingled oak and vine-leaves crowned)
> Would grasp the thyrsus ivy-bound,
> And fold, her festal vest around,
> The Bacchic nebris, leading thus
> The swift and dizzy thiasus:
> And as she moves, in all her charms,
> With springing feet and flowing arms,
> 'Tis strange in one fair shape to see
> How many forms of grace can be.
> The youths and maids, her beauteous train,
> Follow fast in sportive ring,
> Some the torch and mystic cane,
> Some the vine-bough, brandishing;
> Some, in giddy circlets fleeting,
> The Corybantic timbrel beating:
> Maids, with silver flasks advancing,
> Pour the wine's red-sparkling tide,

Which youths, with heads recumbent dancing,
Catch in goblets as they glide:
All upon the odorous air
Lightly toss their leafy hair,
Ever singing, as they move,
   —"Io Bacchus! son of Jove!"—CANTO VII, pp. 148–50.

The Complete Works of Percy Bysshe Shelley, ed. Roger Ingpen and Walter E. Peck (Julian Edition, 10 vols.; New York: Charles Scribner's Sons, 1926–1930), VI, 273–276.

LETTERS

From the Letters

Shelley's letters were valued by his correspondents for many reasons. There were expressions of personal esteem, remarks on business arrangements, passages describing his travels, and records of his associations with people like Byron and Leigh Hunt. Most of all, there was Shelley himself, who expressed himself so naturally and with such evident pleasure in the act of writing that his letters speak from the page. It is hardly possible to know Shelley either as man or as poet without reading his letters. Mary Shelley published a few letters in 1840, but the poet's father prevented her from preparing a full collection or a biography. Shelley's friends, Thomas Jefferson Hogg, Thomas Medwin, Thomas Love Peacock, and Edward John Trelawny, included many of Shelley's letters in their early biographical works, often altering the text to suit their own purposes. In the late nineteenth century, editors and biographers such as H. Buxton Forman and Edward Dowden published additional letters. Roger Ingpen's The Letters of Percy Bysshe Shelley *(1909), the first comprehensive edition, is the principal source of the following passages. In revisions of this work (1912 and 1914), and as co-editor of the Julian Edition (1926-1930), Ingpen was able to add some letters not available to him in 1909, but these include little literary comment. More recently, Professor F. L. Jones has meticulously edited the letters in a nearly complete edition (Oxford: Clarendon Press, 1964). A few letters, held by the Carl H. Pforzheimer Library, could not be included, but they are to be published by that Library. Four of the letters included in the following pages first appeared in publications of Lord Byron's correspondence, and, as indicated in footnotes, are taken from these sources.*

The following passages represent virtually all of the directly critical comments made by Shelley in the published letters. Those of the later years, together with Byron's letters of the same period, are our best insight into the brilliant critical dialogue that centered in these two poets.

Shelley's wide reading has been the subject of special study. References, often merely to author or title, have been indexed in the Julian Edition, Vols. VII and X; in Newman Ivey White's Shelley *(New York: Knopf, 1940);*

in Kenneth Neill Cameron's Young Shelley *(New York: Macmillan, 1950); and in F. L. Jones's edition of* Mary Shelley's Journal *(Norman: University of Oklahoma Press, 1947).*

To Elizabeth Hichener, June 6, 1811

Walter Scott has published a new poem, "The Vision of Don Roderick." I have ordered it. I am not very enthusiastic in the cause of Walter Scott. The aristocratical tone which his writings assume does not prepossess me in his favor, since my opinion is that all poetical beauty ought to be subordinate to the inculcated moral . . . that metaphorical language ought to be a pleasing vehicle for useful and momentous instruction.

To Elizabeth Hichener, July 25, 1811

I am happy that you like "Kehama." Is not the chapter where Kailyal despises the leprosy grand? You would like also "Joan of Arc," by Southey.

To Elizabeth Hichener, December 26, 1811

But Southey, though far from being a man of great reasoning powers, is a great Man. He has all that characterizes the poet,— great eloquence, though obstinacy in opinion, which arguments are the last thing that can shake . . . . He is a man of virtue, he will never belie what he thinks . . . . His professions are in strict compatibility with his practice.

To Lord Byron, July 9, 1817[1]

I have read "Manfred" with the greatest admiration. The same freedom from common rules that marked the third canto [of *Childe Harold*] and "Chillon" is visible here; and it was that which your earlier productions, except "Lara," wanted. But it made me dreadfully melancholy, and I fear other friends in England, too. Why do you indulge this despondency? "Manfred," as far as I learn, is immensely popular; it is characterised as a very daring production.

1. Quoted from *Lord Byron's Correspondence* (London: John Murray, 1922), II, 57–58.

To Thomas Love Peacock, July 12, 1816

I read [Rousseau's] "Julie" all day; an overflowing, as it now seems, surrounded by the scenes which it has so wonderfully peopled, of sublimest genius, and more than human sensibility. Meillerie, the castle of Chillon, Clarens, the mountains of La Valais and Savoy, present themselves to the imagination as monuments of things that were once familiar, and of beings that were once dear to it. They were created indeed by one mind, but a mind so powerfully bright as to cast a shade of falsehood on the records that are called reality.

To a Publisher,[2] *October 13, 1817*

I send you the four first sheets of my poem entitled "Laon and Cythna, or the Revolution of the Golden City."

I believe this commencement affords a sufficient specimen of the work. I am conscious, indeed, that some of the concluding cantos, when "the plot thickens" and human passions are brought into more critical situations of development, are written with more energy and clearness; and that to see a work of which unity is one of the qualifications aimed at by the author in a disjointed state is, in a certain degree, unfavourable to the general impression. If, however, you submit it to Mr. [Thomas] Moore's judgment, he will make due allowance for these circumstances. The whole poem, with the exception of the first canto and part of the last, is a more human story without the smallest intermixture of supernatural interference. The first canto is indeed in some measure a distinct poem, though very necessary to the wholeness of the work. I say this because if it were all written in the manner of the first canto, I could not expect that it would be interesting to any great number of people. I have attempted in the progress of my work to speak to the common elementary emotions of the human heart, so that though it is the story of violence and revolution, it is relieved by milder pictures of friendship and love and natural affections. The scene is supposed to be laid in Constantinople and modern Greece, but without much attempt at minute delineation of Mahometan manners. It is in fact a tale illustrative of such a Revolution as might be supposed to take

2. Probably Longman and Company, publishers of Moore's *Lallah Rookh* (1817).

place in an European nation, acted upon by the opinions of what has been called (erroneously, as I think) the modern philosophy, and contending with ancient notions and the supposed advantage derived from them to those who support them. It is a Revolution of this kind that is the *beau idéal*, as it were, of the French Revolution, but produced by the influence of individual genius and not out of general knowledge. The authors of it are supposed to be my hero and heroine, whose names appear in the title. My private friends have expressed to me a very high, and therefore I do not doubt, a very erroneous judgment of my work. However, of this I can determine neither way. I have resolved to give it a fair chance, and my wish, therefore, is, first, to know whether you would purchase my interest in the copyright—an arrangement which, if there be any truth in the opinions of my friends Lord Byron and Mr. Leigh Hunt of my powers, cannot be disadvantageous to you; and, in the second place, how far you are willing to be the publisher of it on my own account if such an arrangement, which I should infinitely prefer, cannot be made.

To William Godwin, December 11, 1817

I have read and considered all that you say about my general powers, and the particular instance of the poem in which I have attempted to develop them. Nothing can be more satisfactory to me than the interest which your admonitions express. But I think you are mistaken in some points with regard to the peculiar nature of my powers, whatever be their amount. I listened with deference and self-suspicion to your censures of "Laon and Cythna"; but the productions of mine which you commend hold a very low place in my own esteem, and this reassured me, in some degree at least. The poem was produced by a series of thoughts which filled my mind with unbounded and sustained enthusiasm. I felt the precariousness of my life, and I resolved in this book to leave some records of myself. Much of what the volume contains was written with the same feeling, as real, though not so prophetic, as the communications of a dying man. I never presumed, indeed, to consider it anything approaching to faultless; but, when I considered contemporary productions of the same apparent pretensions,

I will own I was filled with confidence. I felt that it was in many respects a genuine picture of my own mind. I felt that the sentiments were true, not assumed; and in this have I long believed that my power consists in sympathy—and that part of imagination which relates to sentiment and contemplation. I am formed, if for anything not in common with the herd of mankind, to apprehend minute and remote distinctions of feeling, whether relative to external nature or the living beings which surround us, and to communicate the conceptions which result from considering either the moral or the material universe as a whole.

To Thomas Love Peacock, April 20, 1818

I have devoted this summer, and indeed the next year, to the composition of a tragedy on the subject of Tasso's madness, which I find upon inspection is, if properly treated, admirably dramatic and poetical.[3] But, you will say, I have no dramatic talent; very true, in a certain sense; but I have taken the resolution to see what kind of a tragedy a person without dramatic talent could write.

To John and Maria Gisborne, July 10, 1818

We have almost finished Ariosto—who is entertaining and graceful, and *sometimes* a poet. Forgive me, worshippers of a more equal and tolerant divinity in poetry, if Ariosto pleases me less than you. Where is the gentle seriousness, the delicate sensibility, the calm and sustained energy, without which true greatness cannot be? He is so cruel, too, in his descriptions; his most prized virtues are vices almost without disguise. He constantly vindicates and embellishes revenge in its grossest form; the most deadly superstition that ever infested the world. How different from the tender and solemn enthusiasm of Petrarch—or even the delicate moral sensibility of Tasso, though somewhat obscured by an assumed and artificial style.

To Thomas Love Peacock, August 16, 1818

What a wonderful passage there is in [Plato's] "Phoedrus"—the beginning, I think, of one of the speeches of Socrates—in praise of

3. Of Shelley's attempt to dramatize this subject only a short scene and a song remain (*The Complete Poetical Works of Percy Bysshe Shelley*, ed. Thomas Hutchinson [London: Oxford University Press, 1904], 554–555).

poetic madness, and in definition of what poetry is, and how a man becomes a poet. Every man who lives in this age and desires to write poetry, ought, as a preservative against the false and narrow systems of criticism which every poetical empiric vents, to impress himself with this sentence, if he would be numbered among those to whom may apply this proud, though sublime expression of Tasso: "None merits the name of creator but God and the poet." [4]

To Thomas Love Peacock, December 22, 1818

I entirely agree with what you say about "Childe Harold." The spirit in which it is written is, if insane, the most wicked and mischievous insanity that ever was given forth. It is a kind of obstinate and self-willed folly, in which he hardens himself.

To Thomas Love Peacock, January 26, 1819

I consider poetry very subordinate to moral and political science, and if I were well, certainly I would aspire to the latter; for I can conceive a great work, embodying the discoveries of all ages, and harmonising the contending creeds by which mankind have been ruled.

To Thomas Love Peacock, June 20 [?], 1819

I am delighted with "Nightmare Abbey." I think Scythrop a character admirably conceived and executed; and I know not how to praise sufficiently the lightness, chastity, and strength of the language of the whole. It perhaps exceeds all your other works in this. The catastrophe is excellent. I suppose the moral is contained in what Falstaff says—"For God's sake, talk like a man of this world"; and yet, looking deeper into it, is not the misdirected enthusiasm of Scythrop what J. C. calls the "salt of the earth"?

To Thomas Love Peacock, July 1819

The object of the present letter is to ask a favor of you. I have written a tragedy [The Cenci], on the subject of a story well known in Italy, and, in my conception, eminently dramatic. I have taken some

4. "*Non che in mondo chi merita nome di creatore, che Dio ed il Poeta.*" A variant of this passage is cited by Shelley in "A Defence of Poetry," and also in "Essay on Life." See *Shelley's Prose*, ed. David Lee Clark (Albuquerque: University of New Mexico Press, 1954), p. 172.

pains to make my play fit for representation, and those who have already seen it judge favorably. It is written without any of the peculiar feelings and opinions which characterize my other compositions; I having attended simply to the impartial development of such characters as it is probable the persons represented really were, together with the greatest degree of popular effect to be produced by such a development. I send you a translation of the Italian manuscript on which my play is founded, the chief subject of which I have touched very delicately; for my principal doubt, as to whether such a thing as incest in this shape, however treated, would be admitted on the stage. I think, however, it will form no objection: considering, first, that the facts are a matter of history; and secondly, the peculiar delicacy with which I have treated it.

I am exceedingly interested in the question of whether this attempt of mine will succeed or no. I am strongly inclined to the affirmative at present, founding my hopes on this, that, as a composition, it is certainly not inferior to any of the modern plays that have been acted, with the exception of "Remorse"; that the interest of its plot is incredibly greater and more real; and that there is nothing beyond what the multitude are contented to believe that they can understand, either in imagery, opinion, or sentiment. I wish to preserve a complete incognito, and can trust to you, that whatever else you do, you will at least favor me on this point. Indeed this is essential, deeply essential to its success. After it had been acted, and successfully (could I hope such a thing), I would own it if I pleased, and use the celebrity it might acquire to my own purposes.

What I want you to do is, to procure for me its presentation at Covent Garden. The principal character, Beatrice, is precisely fitted for Miss O'Neil, and it might even seem written for her (God forbid that I should ever see her play it—it would tear my nerves to pieces,) and, in all respects, it is fitted only for Covent Garden. The chief male character, I confess, I should be very unwilling that anyone but Kean[5] should play—that is impossible, and I must be

5. Miss Eliza O'Neil had attracted Shelley's interest when he saw her in Milman's *Fazio*, February 16, 1818. Edmund Kean (1787–1833) was one of the great tragic actors of the period.

contented with an inferior actor. I think you know some of the people of that theatre, or, at least, some one who knows them; and when you have read the play, you may say enough, perhaps, to induce them not to reject it without consideration—but of this, perhaps, I may judge from the tragedies which they have accepted, there is no danger at any rate.

Write to me as soon as you can on this subject, because it is necessary that I should present it, or, if rejected by the theatre, print it this coming season; lest somebody else should get hold of it, as the story, which now only exists in manuscript, begins to be generally known among the English. The translation which I send you is to be prefixed to the play, together with a print of Beatrice. I have a copy of her picture by Guido, now in the Colonna palace at Rome—the most beautiful creature, you can conceive.[6]

To Leigh Hunt, August 15, 1819

I send you a little poem [*Julian and Maddalo: A Conversation*] to give to Ollier for publication, but *without my name*. Peacock will correct the proofs. I wrote it with the idea of offering it to the *Examiner*, but I find that it is too long. It was composed last year at Este; two of the characters you will recognize; the third is also in some degree a painting from nature, but, with respect to time and place, ideal. You will find the little piece, I think, in some degree consistent with your own ideas of the manner in which poetry ought to be written. I have employed a certain familiar style of language to express the actual way in which people talk with each other, whom education and a certain refinement of sentiment have placed above the use of the vulgar idioms. I use the word *vulgar* in its most extensive sense. The vulgarity of rank and fashion is as gross in its way as that of Poverty, and its cant terms equally expressive of bare conceptions, and therefore equally unfit for Poetry. Not that the familiar style is to be admitted in the treatment of a subject wholly ideal, or in that part of any subject which relates

6. The portrait is reproduced in *The Letters of Percy Bysshe Shelley*, ed. Roger Ingpen (2 vols.; London: Sir Isaac Pitman and Sons, Ltd., 1909), II, 700, with the explanation that it was not by Guido, as Shelley thought. The translation of the story was published by Mary Shelley in her edition of Shelley's *Poetical Works* (1839), but is not included in the Julian Edition.

to common life, where the passion, exceeding a certain limit, touches the boundaries of that which is ideal. Strong passion expresses itself in metaphor, borrowed from subjects alike remote or near, and casts over all the shadow of its own greatness.

To Leigh Hunt, September 3, 1819

With it came, too, Lamb's Works.—I have looked at none of the other books yet.—What a lovely thing is his "Rosamund Gray," how much knowledge of the sweetest and deepest parts of our nature is in it! When I think of such a mind as Lamb's—when I see how unnoticed remain things of such exquisite and complete perfection, what should I hope for myself, if I had not higher objects in view than fame?

To Charles and James Ollier, September 6, 1819

[Of Keats's *Endymion*] . . . much praise is due to me for having read it, the author's intention appearing to be that no person should possibly get to the end of it. Yet it is full of some of the highest and finest gleams of poetry; indeed, everything seems to be viewed by the mind of a poet which is described in it. I think if he had printed about fifty pages of fragments from it, I should have been led to admire Keats as a poet more than I ought, of which there is now no danger.

To Thomas Love Peacock, September 21, 1819

Charles Clairmont is now with us on his way to Vienna. He has spent a year or more in Spain, where he has learnt Spanish, and I make him read Spanish all day long. It is a most powerful and expressive language, and I have already learnt sufficient to read with great ease their poet Calderón. I have read about 12 of his plays. Some of them certainly deserve to be ranked among the grandest and most perfect productions of the human mind. He exceeds all modern dramatists, with the exception of Shakespeare, whom he resembles, however, in the depth of thought and subtlety of imagination of his writings, and in the rare power of interweaving delicate and powerful comic traits with the most tragical situations, without diminishing their interest. I rate him far above Beaumont and Fletcher.

To Leigh Hunt, September 27, 1819

[Of Boccaccio] I have been lately reading this most divine writer. He is, in a high sense of the word, a poet, and his language has the rhythm and harmony of verse. I think him not equal certainly to Dante or Petrarch, but far superior to Tasso and Ariosto, the children of a later and of a colder day. ... When the second-rate poets of Italy wrote, the corrupting blight of tyranny was already hanging on every bud of genius. Energy, and simplicity, and unity of idea, were no more. ... How much do I admire Boccaccio! What descriptions of nature are those in his little introductions to every new day! It is the morning of life stripped of that mist of familiarity which makes it obscure to us.

To Charles and James Ollier, October 15, 1819

The "Prometheus," a poem in my best style, whatever that may amount to, will arrive with it, but in MS., which you can print and publish in the season. It is the most perfect of my productions.

To Leigh Hunt, November 2, 1819

[Shelley requests that *Peter Bell the Third* be published anonymously.] My motive in this is solely not to prejudice myself in the present moment, as I have only expended a few days in this party squib, and, of course, taken little pains. The verses and language I have let come as they would, and I am about to publish more serious things this winter: afterwards, that is next year, if the thing be remembered so long, I have no objection to the author being known, but *not now*.

To Maria Gisborne, November 16, 1819

I have been reading Calderón without you. I have read the "Cisma de Ingalaterra," the "Cabellos de Absolom," and three or four others. These pieces, inferior to those we read, at least to the "Principe Constante," in the splendour of particular passages, are perhaps superior in their satisfying completeness. The "Cabellos de Absolom" is full of the deepest and tenderest touches of nature. Nothing can be more pathetically conceived than the character of old David, and the tender and impartial love, overcoming all insults and all crimes, with which he regards his conflicting and disobedient sons. The incest scene of Amnon and Tamar is perfectly tremendous. Well may Calderón say in the person of the former:—

> If blood without fire wounds
> what will blood with fire do?[7]

Incest is, like many other incorrect things, a very poetical circumstance. It may be the excess of love or hate. It may be the defiance of everything for the sake of another, which clothes itself in the glory of the highest heroism; or it may be that cynical rage which, confounding the good and the bad in existing opinions, breaks through them for the purpose of rioting in selfishness and antipathy. Calderón, following the Jewish historians, has represented Amnon's action in the basest point of view—he is a prejudiced savage, acting what he abhors, and abhorring that which is the unwilling party to his crime.

To Charles and James Ollier, March 6, 1820

"Prometheus Unbound," I must tell you, is my favorite poem; I charge you, therefore, especially to pet him and feed him with fine ink and good paper. "Cenci" is written for the multitude, and ought to sell well. I think, if I may judge by its merits, the "Prometheus" cannot sell beyond twenty copies.

To Lord Byron, May 26, 1820[8]

I have read your "Don Juan" [Cantos I and II] in print, and I observe that the *murrain* has killed some of the finest of the flock, i.e., that your bookseller has omitted certain passages. The personal ones, however, though I thought them wonderfully strong, I do not regret. What a strange and terrible storm is that at sea, and the two fathers, how true, yet how strong a contrast! Dante hardly exceeds it. With what flashes of divine beauty have you not illuminated the familiarity of your subject towards the end! The love letter, and the account of its being written, is altogether a masterpiece of portraiture; of human nature laid with the eternal colours of the feelings of humanity. Where did you learn all these secrets?

7. *Si sangre sin fuego hiere*
   que fara sangre con fuego?
8. Quoted from *Lord Byron's Correspondence*, II, 149–151.

I should like to go to school there. I cannot say I equally approve of the service to which this letter was appropriated; or that I altogether think the bitter mockery of our common nature, of which this is one of the expressions, quite worthy of your genius. The power and the beauty and the wit, indeed, redeem all this—chiefly because they belie and refute it. Perhaps it is foolish to wish that there had been nothing to redeem. My tragedy [*The Cenci*] you will find less horrible than you had reason to expect. At all events it is matter-of-fact. If I had known you would have liked to have seen it, I could have sent you a copy, for I printed it in Italy, and sent it to England for publication. Did you see a little poem called "Rosalind and Helen" of mine? It was a mere extempore thing, and worth little, I believe. If you wish to see it, I can send it you.

To John Keats, July 27, 1820[9]

I hear with great pain the dangerous accident that you have undergone, and Mr. Gisborne who gives me the account of it, adds that you continue to wear a consumptive appearance. This consumption is a disease particularly fond of people who write such good verses as you have done, and with the assistance of an English winter it can often indulge its selection;—I do not think that young and amiable poets are at all bound to gratify its taste; they have entered into no bond with the Muses to that effect. But seriously (for I am joking on what I am very anxious about) I think you would do well to pass the winter after so tremendous an accident, in Italy, and if you think it as necessary as I do so long as you could [find] Pisa or its neighborhood agreeable to you, Mrs. Shelley unites with myself in urging the request, that you would take up your residence with us. You might come by sea to Leghorn (France is not worth seeing, and the sea is particularly good for weak lungs), which is within a few miles of us. You ought at all events, to see Italy, and your health, which I suggest as a motive, might be an excuse to you. I spare declamation about the statues, and the paintings, and the ruins—and what is a greater piece of forbearance—about the

9. Keats's reply, written from Hampstead in August, is given in most collections of his letters, and is reprinted in *The Letters of Percy Bysshe Shelley*, ed. Ingpen, II, 810.

mountains and streams and fields, the colours of the sky, and the sky itself.

I have lately read your "Endymion" again and ever with a new sense of the treasures of poetry it contains, though treasures poured forth with indistinct profusion. This, people in general will not endure, and that is the cause of the comparatively few copies which have been sold. I feel persuaded that you are capable of the greatest things, so you but will.

I always tell Ollier to send you copies of my books.—"Prometheus Unbound" I imagine you will receive nearly at the same time with this letter. "The Cenci" I hope you have already received—it was studiously composed in a different style

"Below the *good* how far! but far above the *great*." [10]

In poetry I have sought to avoid system and mannerism; I wish those who excel me in genius would pursue the same plan.

Whether you remain in England, or journey to Italy,—believe that you carry with you my anxious wishes for your health, happiness and success wherever you are, or whatever you undertake, and that I am, yours sincerely,

To Thomas Love Peacock, November 8 [?], 1820

Among the modern things which have reached me is a volume of poems by Keats; in other respects insignificant enough, but containing the fragment of a poem called "Hyperion." I dare say you have not time to read it; but it is certainly an astonishing piece of writing, and gives me a conception of Keats which I confess I had not before.

To the Editor of the Quarterly Review, *November, 1820* [11]

Should you cast your eye on the signature of this letter before you read the contents you might imagine that they related to a slanderous paper which appeared in your review some time since. I never notice

10. Thomas Gray, "The Progress of Poesy," l. 122. This final line usually appears: "Below the *Good* how far—but far above the *Great*."

11. This letter was never sent to William Gifford, then editor of the *Quarterly Review*, which had published attacks on Keats's *Endymion* (April, 1818), and on Shelley's *The Revolt of Islam* (April, 1819).

anonymous attacks. The wretch who wrote it has doubtless the additional reward of a consciousness of his motives, besides the 30 guineas a sheet, or whatever it is that you pay him. Of course you cannot be answerable for all the writings which you edit, and *I* certainly bear you no ill will for having edited the abuse to which I allude—indeed, I was too much amused by being compared to Pharaoh not readily to forgive editor printer publisher stitcher or any one, except the despicable writer, connected with something so exquisitely entertaining. Seriously speaking, I am not in the habit of permitting myself to be disturbed by what is said or written of me, though, I dare say, I may be condemned sometimes justly enough. But I feel, in respect to the writer in question, that "I am there sitting, where he durst not soar."

The case is different with the unfortunate subject of this letter, the author of Endymion, to whose feelings and situation I entreat you to allow me to call your attention. I write considerably in the dark, but if it is Mr. Gifford that I am addressing, I am persuaded that in an appeal to his humanity and justice, he will acknowledge the right to learn from the stranger.[12] I am aware that the first duty of a Reviewer is towards the public, and I am willing to confess that the Endymion is a poem considerably defective, and that, perhaps, it deserved as much censure as the pages of your *Review* record against it. But, not to mention that there is certain contemptuousness of phraseology from which it is difficult for a critic to abstain, in the Review of Endymion I do not think that the writer has given it its due praise. Surely the poem with all its faults is a very remarkable production for a man of Keats's age and the promise of ultimate excellence is such as has rarely been afforded even by such as have afterwards attained high literary eminence. Look at Book 2, line 833, etc., and Book 3, line 113 to 120—read down that page, and then again from line 193. I could cite many other passages, to convince you that it deserved milder usage. Why it should have been reviewed at all, excepting for the purpose of bringing its excellences into notice I cannot conceive, for it was very little read, and there was no danger that it should become a model to the age of that false taste, with which I confess that it is replenished.

12. *"fas ab hoste doceri."*

Poor Keats was thrown into a dreadful state of mind by this review, which, I am persuaded, was not written with any intention of producing the effect to which it has at least greatly contributed, of embittering his existence, and inducing a disease from which there are now but faint hopes of his recovery. The first effects are described to me to have resembled insanity, and it was by assiduous watching that he was restrained from effecting purposes of suicide. The agony of his sufferings at length produced the rupture of a blood-vessel in the lungs, and the usual process of consumption appears to have begun. He is coming to pay me a visit in Italy; but I fear that unless his mind can be kept tranquil, little is to be hoped from the mere influence of climate.

But let me not extort anything from your pity. I have just seen a second volume published by him evidently in careless despair. I have desired my bookseller to send you a copy, and allow me to solicit your especial attention to the fragment of a poem entitled Hyperion, the composition of which was checked by the Review in question. The great proportion of this piece is surely in the very highest style of poetry. I speak impartially, for the canons of taste to which Keats has conformed in his other compositions are the very reverse of my own. I leave you to judge for yourself: it would be an insult to you to suppose that from motives, however honourable, you would lend yourself to a deception of the public.

To Charles Ollier, February 16, 1821

The longer poem [*Epipsychidion*], I desire, should not be considered my own; indeed, in a certain sense, it is a production of a portion of me already dead; and in this sense the advertisement [13] is no fiction.

To Lord Byron, April 16, 1821 [14]

I see by the papers that you have published a tragedy [*Marino Faliero*] on the subject of which you spoke when I saw you at Venice. I have not yet seen it, though I am most anxious to observe this new phasis of your power. The last work of yours I have seen is "Don Juan," in the poetical parts of which you seem to have equalled the finest passages in your former poems; except the *curse*

13. See above, pp. 70–71.
14. Quoted from *Lord Byron's Correspondence*, II, 168–169.

in "Manfred," the stanzas in Chillon in the third, and the address to Ocean in the fourth canto of "Childe Harold." You have now arrived about at the age at which those eternal poets, of whom we have authentic accounts, have ever begun their supreme poems; considering all their others, however transcendent, as the steps, the scaffolding, the exercise which may sustain and conduct them to their great work. If you are inferior to these, it is not in genius, but industry and resolution. Oh, that you would subdue yourself to the great task of building up a poem containing within itself the germs of a permanent relation to the present, and to all succeeding ages!

Young Keats, whose "Hyperion" showed so great a promise, died lately at Rome from the consequences of breaking a blood-vessel, in paroxysms of despair at the contemptuous attack on his book in the *Quarterly Review*.

To Henry Reveley, April 19, 1821

Tell Mr. and Mrs. Gisborne that I have read the "Numancia" [by Cervantes], and after wading through the singular stupidity of the first act, began to be greatly delighted, and, at length, interested to a very high degree, by the power of the writer in awakening pity and admiration, in which I hardly know by whom he is excelled. There is little, I allow, in a strict sense, to be called *poetry* in this play; but the command of language, and the harmony of versification, is so great as to deceive one into an idea that it is poetry.

To John and Maria Gisborne, June 5, 1821

I have been engaged these last days in composing a poem on the death of Keats, which will shortly be finished; and I anticipate the pleasure of reading it to you, as some of the very few persons who will be interested in it and understand it. It is a highly-wrought *piece of art*, and perhaps better, in point of composition, than anything I have written.

To Charles Ollier, June 8, 1821

You may announce for publication a poem entitled "Adonais." It is a lament on the death of poor Keats, with some interposed stabs on the assassins of his peace and of his fame; and will be preceded by a criticism on "Hyperion," asserting the due claims which that fragment gives him to the rank which I have assigned him.

To Charles Ollier, June 11, 1821

I hear that a bookseller of the name of Clark has published a poem which I wrote in early youth, called "Queen Mab" [1812–1813]. I have not seen it for some years, but inasmuch as I recollect it is villainous trash; and I daresay much better fitted to injure than to serve the cause which it advocates.

To Mary Wollstonecraft Shelley, August 7, 1821

Conversation with Lord Byron. We talked a great deal of poetry, and such matters last night; and as usual differed, and I think more than ever. He affects to patronise a system of criticism fit for the production of mediocrity, and although all his fine poems and passages have been produced in defiance of this system, yet I recognize the pernicious effects of it in "The Doge of Venice"; and it will cramp and limit his future efforts, however great they may be, unless he gets rid of it. I have read only parts of it, or rather he himself read them to me, and gave me the plan of the whole.

To John Gisborne, June 16, 1821

A droll circumstance has occurred. "Queen Mab," a poem written by me when very young, in the most furious style, with long notes against Jesus Christ, and God the Father, and the King, and bishops, and marriage, and the devil knows what, is just published by one of the low booksellers in the Strand, against my wish and consent, and all the people are at loggerheads about it. Horace Smith gives me this account. You may imagine how much I am amused. For the sake of dignified appearance, however, and really because I wish to protest against all the bad poetry in it, I have given orders to say that it is all done against my desire, and have directed my attorney to apply to Chancery for an injunction, which he will not get.

To Thomas Love Peacock, August 10, 1821

I received your last letter just as I was setting off from the Bagni on a visit to Lord Byron at this place. Many thanks for all your kind attention to my accursed affairs. . . .

I have sent you by the Gisbornes a copy of the *Elegy on Keats*. The subject, I know, will not please you; but the composition of the poetry, and the taste in which it is written, I do not think bad. You and the enlightened public will judge. Lord Byron is in excellent cue both of health and spirits. He has got rid of all those melancholy and degrading habits which he indulged [in] at Venice. He lives with one woman, a lady of rank here, to whom he is attached, and who is attached to him, and is in every respect an altered man. He has written three more cantos of "Don Juan." I have yet only heard the fifth, and I think that every word of it is pregnant with immortality. I have not seen his late plays, except "Marino Faliero," which is very well, but not so transcendently fine as the "Don Juan." . . . Lord B. thinks you wrote a pamphlet signed "John Bull"; [15] he says he knew it by the style resembling "Melincourt," of which he is a great admirer. I read it, and assured him that it could not possibly be yours. I write nothing, and probably shall write no more. It offends me to see my name classed among those who have no name. If I cannot be something better, I had rather be nothing, and the accursed cause to the downfall of which I dedicated what powers I may have had—flourishes like a cedar and covers England with its boughs. My motive was never the infirm desire of fame; and if I should continue an author, I feel that I should [not?] desire it. This cup is justly given to one only of an age; indeed, participation would make it worthless: and unfortunate they who seek it and find it not.

To Mary Wollstonecraft Shelley, August 10, 1821

He [Byron] has read to me one of the unpublished cantos of "Don Juan" [Canto V], which is astonishingly fine. It sets him not only above, but far above, all the poets of the day—every word is stamped with immortality. I despair of rivalling Lord Byron, as well I may, and there is no other with whom it is worth contending. This canto is in the style, but totally, and sustained with incredible ease and power, like the end of the second canto. There is not a word which the most rigid asserter of the dignity of human nature would desire to be cancelled. It fulfils, in a certain degree, what I

15. Peacock denied authorship of the pamphlet.

have long preached of producing—something wholly new and relative to the age, and yet surpassingly beautiful. It may be vanity, but I think I see the trace of my earnest exhortations to him to create something wholly new.

To Mary Wollstonecraft Shelley, August 11, 1821

I am reading "Anastasius." [16] One would think that Lord Byron had taken his idea of the three last cantos of "Don Juan" from this book. That, of course, has nothing to do with the merit of this latter, poetry having nothing to do with the invention of facts. It is a very powerful, and a very entertaining novel, and a faithful picture, they say, of modern Greek manners. I have read Lord Byron's letter to Bowles: some good things—but he ought not to write prose criticism.

To Lord Byron, October 21, 1821 [17]

I should have written to you long since but that I have been led to expect you almost daily in Pisa, and that I imagined you would cross my letter on your road.—Many thanks for "Don Juan" [Cantos III–V]—It is a poem totally of its own species, and my wonder and delight at the grace of the composition no less than the free and grand vigour of the conception of it perpetually increase.— The few passages which anyone might desire to be cancelled in the first and second cantos are here reduced almost to nothing. The poem carries with it at once the stamp of originality and a defiance of imitation. Nothing has ever been written like it in English— nor if I may venture to prophesy, will there be; without carrying upon it the mark of a secondary and borrowed light.—You unveil and present in its true deformity what is worst in human nature, and this is what the witlings of the age murmur at, conscious of their want of power to endure the scrutiny of such a light.—We are damned to the knowledge of good and evil, and it is well for us to know what we should avoid no less than what we should seek.

16. *Anastasius, or Memoirs of a Greek Written at the Close of the Eighteenth Century* (1819), a novel by Thomas Hope (1770–1831). It was praised by Byron, and favorably reviewed by Sydney Smith in the *Edinburgh Review* (1821).
17. Quoted from *The Works of Lord Byron: Letters and Journals* (London: John Murray, 1901), V, 389–390.

—The character of Lambro—his return—the merriment of his daughters' guests made as it were in celebration of his funeral—the meeting with the lovers—and the death of Haidée—are circumstances combined and developed in a manner that I seek elsewhere in vain. The fifth canto, which some of your pet Zoili in Albemarle St. said was *dull*, gathers instead of loses, splendour and energy— the language in which the whole is clothed—a sort of chameleon under the changing sky of the spirit that kindles it—is such as these lisping days could not have expected,—and are, believe me, in spite of their approbation which you wrest from them—little pleased to hear.

One can hardly judge from recitation, and it was not until I read it in print that I have been able to do it justice.—This sort of writing only on a great plan, and perhaps in a more compact form, is what I wished you to do when I made my vows for an epic.

—But I am content—You are building up a drama, such as England has not yet seen, and the task is sufficiently noble and worthy of you.

To John Gisborne, October 22, 1821

The Epipsychidion is a mystery; as to real flesh and blood, you know that I do not deal in those articles; you might as well go to a gin-shop for a leg of mutton, as expect anything human or earthly from me. . . .

I read the Greek dramatists and Plato forever. You are right about Antigone; how sublime a picture of a woman! and what think you of the choruses, and especially the lyrical complaints of the godlike victim? and the menaces of Tiresias, and their rapid fulfillment? Some of us have, in a prior existence, been in love with an Antigone, and that makes us find no full content in any mortal tie. As to books, I advise you to live near the British Museum, and read there. I have read, since I saw you, the "Jungfrau von Orleans" of Schiller,—a fine play, if the fifth act did not fall off.

To Jospeh Severn, November 29, 1821

I send you the elegy on poor Keats—and I wish it were better worth your acceptance. You will see, by the preface, that it was written before I could obtain any particular account of his last moments; all that I still know, was communicated to me by a

friend who had derived his information from Colonel Finch; I
have ventured to express, as I felt, the respect and admiration
which *your* conduct towards him demands.

In spite of his transcendent genius, Keats never was, nor ever will
be, a popular poet; and the total neglect and obscurity in which the
astonishing remnants of his mind still lie, was hardly to be dis-
sipated by a writer, who, however he may differ from Keats in
more important qualities, at least resembles him in that accidental
one, a want of popularity.

I have little hope, therefore, that the poem I send you will excite
any attention, nor do I feel assured that a critical notice of his
writings would find a single reader. But for these considerations, it
had been my intention to have collected the remnants of his
compositions, and to have published them with a life and criticism.
—Has he left any poems or writings of whatsoever kind, and in
whose possession are they? Perhaps you will oblige me by information
on this point.

Many thanks for the picture you promised me: I shall consider
it amongst the most sacred relics of the past.

For my part, I little expected, when I last saw Keats at my
friend Leigh Hunt's, that I should survive him.[18]

To John Gisborne, April 10, 1822

I have received "Hellas," which is prettily printed, and with
fewer mistakes than any poem I ever published. Am I to thank you
for the revision of the press? or who acted as midwife to this last of
my orphans, introducing it to oblivion, and me to my accustomed
failure? May the cause it celebrates be more fortunate than either!
Tell me how you like "Hellas," and give me your opinion freely.
It was written without much care, and in one of those few moments
of enthusiasm which now seldom visit me, and which make me pay
dear for their visits. I know what to think of "Adonais," but what to
think of those who confound it with the many bad poems of the day,
I know not.

I have been reading over and over again "Faust," and always
with sensations which no other composition excites. It deepens the

18. Shelley first met Keats at Leigh Hunt's in December, 1816. Shelley left
England in March, 1818.

gloom and augments the rapidity of ideas, and would therefore seem to me an unfit study for any person who is a prey to the reproaches of memory, and the delusions of an imagination not to be restrained. And yet the pleasure of sympathizing with emotions known only to few, although they derive their sole charm from despair, and the scorn of the narrow good we can attain in our present state, seems more than to ease the pain which belongs to them. Perhaps all discontent with the *less* (to use a Platonic sophism) supposes the sense of a just claim to the *greater*, and that we admirers of "Faust" are on the right road to Paradise. Such a supposition is not more absurd, and is certainly less demoniacal, than that of Wordsworth, where he says—

> This earth,
> Which is the world of all of us, and where
> *We find our happiness, or not at all.*[19]

As if, after sixty years' suffering here, we were to be roasted alive for sixty million more in hell, or charitably annihilated by a *coup de grâce* of the bungler who brought us into existence at first!

Have you read Calderón's "Magico Prodigioso"? I find a striking similarity between "Faust" and this drama, and if I were to acknowledge Coleridge's distinction, should say Goethe was the *greatest* philosopher, Calderón the *greatest* poet. "Cyprian" evidently furnished the *germ* of "Faust," as "Faust" may furnish the germ of other poems; although it is as different from it in structure and plan as the acorn from the oak. I have—imagine my presumption—translated several scenes from both, as the basis of a paper for your journal. I am well content with those from Calderón, which in fact gave me very little trouble; but those from "Faust"—I feel how imperfect a representation, even with all the licence I assumed to figure to myself how Goethe would have written in English, my words convey. No one but Coleridge is capable of such work.

19. *The Prelude*, XI, 142–144. The passage, first published in *The Friend*, October 26, 1809, entitled "French Revolution, as It Appeared to Enthusiasts at Its Commencement"; it was reprinted in the 1815 edition of Wordsworth's poems. The italics in the quoted lines are Shelley's.

We have seen here a translation of some scenes, and indeed the most remarkable ones, accompanying those astonishing etchings which have been published in England from a German master.[20] It is not bad—and faithful enough—but how weak! how incompetent to represent Faust! I have only attempted the scenes omitted in this translation, and would send you that of the "Walpurgisnacht," if I thought Ollier would place the postage to my account. What etchings those are! I am never satiated with looking at them; and, I fear, it is the only sort of translation of which "Faust" is susceptible. I never perfectly understood the Hartz Mountain scene, until I saw the etching; and then, Margaret in the summer-house with Faust! The artist makes one envy his happiness that he can sketch such things with calmness, which I only dared look upon once, and which made my brain swim round only to touch the leaf on the opposite side of which I knew that it was figured. Whether it is that the artist has surpassed "Faust," or that the pencil surpasses language in some subjects, I know not, or that I am more affected by a visible image, but the etching certainly excited me far more than the poem it illustrated. Do you remember the fifty-fourth letter of the first part of the "Nouvelle Héloïse"? Goethe, in a subsequent scene, evidently had that letter in his mind, and this etching is an idealism of it. So much for the world of shadows.

What think you of Lord Byron's last volume?[21] In my opinion it contains finer poetry than has appeared in England since the publication of "Paradise Regained." "Cain" is apocalyptic—it is a revelation not before communicated to man. I write nothing but by fits. I have done some of "Charles I"; but although the poetry succeeded very well, I cannot seize on the conception of the subject as a whole. You know I don't think much about Reviews, nor of the fame they give, nor of that they take away. It is absurd in any Review to criticise "Adonais," and still more to pretend that the

20. The etchings were by Friederich August Moritz Retzsch. The summer-house scene, mentioned by Shelley, is reproduced in *The Letters of Percy Bysshe Shelley*, ed. Ingpen, II, 954.

21. *Sardanapalus, A Tragedy. The Two Foscari, A Tragedy. Cain, A Mystery*, published in a single volume (1821).

verses are bad. "Prometheus" was never intended for more than five or six persons.[22]

Except where otherwise specified, all the passages from Shelley's correspondence in this section are taken from *The Letters of Percy Bysshe Shelley*, ed. Roger Ingpen (2 vols.; London: Sir Isaac Pitman and Sons, Ltd., 1909; rev. ed., 1915), I, 90, 120, 200; II, 496–497, 558–559, 573–574, 595–596, 603–604, 615, 650–651, 660, 694, 697–699, 705–706, 711–712, 715–716, 719, 721, 728, 735, 749–750, 766, 808–810, 828–830, 849, 866, 871–872, 874, 875–876, 877, 888, 894, 896–898, 899, 920, 921, 922–923, 953–955.

22. The last paragraph is printed by Jones as a part of Shelley's letter to Gisborne dated January 26 (*The Letters of Percy Bysshe Shelley*, ed. F. L. Jones [2 vols.; Oxford: Oxford University Press, 1964], II, 388).

APPENDICES

Appendix A
Byron and Shelley on the
Character of Hamlet

This dialogue appeared anonymously in 1830 in the New Monthly Magazine and Literary Journal,[1] *and has never previously been reprinted entire. Walter E. Peck's* Shelley, His Life and Work[2] *includes an abbreviated version from* The Polar Star[3] *which bore the subcaption "By an Eye Witness"; Peck, in a footnote, adds "Possibly Thomas Medwin."*

In a recent essay, "Shelley's Last Poetics,"[4] Earl R. Wasserman accepts the dialogue as probably genuine. Wasserman recalls a passage in Samuel Rogers' Table Talk *which mentions a Pisan dinner conversation on Shakespeare between Byron and Shelley. Wasserman also points out that the literary allusions attributed to Shelley in the dialogue are to Shelley's favorite authors, and that the argument is an application of views expressed in Shelley's "Defence of Poetry" and in other writings.*

Such evidence is not conclusive, of course. If Medwin was the anonymous reporter of the dialogue, it is strange that he did not include it or allude to it in his Life of Shelley (1874). *If Edward John Trelawny was present at the dinner in Pisa alluded to by Samuel Rogers, and later published the dialogue, why is there no mention of it in his* Recollections of the Last Days of Shelley and Byron (1858)? *Another of Shelley's friends, Thomas Jefferson Hogg, contributed reminiscences of Shelley to the* New Monthly Magazine *in 1832, but Hogg had little contact with Shelley after 1818. If, however, neither Medwin, nor Trelawny, nor Hogg contributed the*

1. N.S. XXIX, pt. ii, 327–336.
2. Boston and New York: Houghton Mifflin, 1927, II, 421–435.
3. July–October, 1830.
4. In *From Sensibility to Romanticism*, ed. Frederick W. Hilles and Harold Bloom (New York: Oxford University Press, 1965), pp. 487–511.

dialogue, who could have reported—or invented—it? The question of authorship merits further attention. Meanwhile, the views expressed are interesting for their close correspondence to Shelley's known opinions. As Wasserman points out, the conclusion attributed to Shelley is an echo of the doctrine of the then unpublished "Defence of Poetry": *"It appears, therefore, that Hamlet is, in itself, a complete and reasonable whole, composed in an harmonious proportion of difference and similitude, into one expressive unity."*

It was indeed a delightful day. We had spent the hot time under some of the old, over-canopying chesnuts of the Grand Duke's wood; and perceiving now the green and golden light of sunset through the valleys of tree-tops, we began to wind our way home through the wilderness of underwood, following the track of a little path or sheepwalk, which led through the forest, as it gradually opened, and ended in the stately avenue of the Grand Duke's palace. Here, in the wide space, under those lofty trees, we were no longer constrained to walk singly, and Shelley placed himself beside Lord Byron, who led the way through the trees: "You seem very ineffable this evening," said he.

"I have been reading," he replied, "Hamlet."

"No wonder then you are melancholy."

"No," said Lord Byron, "'tis not so much melancholy, but I feel perplexed, confused, and inextricably self-involved; a nightmare sensation of impotence and vain endeavour weighs upon me, whether my own or Shakespeare's. Nor do I at all recognize in my feelings that calmness and grandeur which you said the other day one always felt in the presence of great genius."

Shelley. I understand you! 'Tis a feeling one but too often feels; when an object stands before one, unintelligible, "wrapped in its own formless horror like a ghost."

Byron. I don't wonder you quote that line of yours. It is one of the best you ever wrote. I think it great affectation not to quote oneself.

Shelley. But you must not let Hamlet pass. Pray go on with your observations upon it, if not disagreeable.

Byron. It takes some time for one's feelings to form themselves into any definite and expressible shapes—just as they say that it takes three days for the rain-water to get to the rivers—one for the ground, one for the drains, and one for the ditches; and it is very hard of any one to come as you do now, and trampling over one's feelings, while they are yet soft with the drenching of your Castalian dew, to stamp uneffaceably the impression of the moment.

Shelley. Oh, I assure you we won't print you down at your word. You may say just the contrary, if it please your Lordship, tomorrow; but sufficient for the evening is the opinion thereof.

Byron. Why, believe me, I have no opinion of any sort. If I had but an opinion—what can any man want more? But now I am like a nothing, a want, a privation. What *is* Hamlet? What means he? Are we, too, like him, the creatures of some incomprehensible sport, and the real universe just such another story, where all the deepest feelings, and dearest sympathies are insulted, and the understanding mocked? And yet we live on, as we read on, for

—————Who would lose
Though full of pain, this intellectual being,
These thoughts that wander through eternity? [5]

And who can read this wonderful play without the profoundest emotion? And yet what is it but a colossal enigma? We love Hamlet even as we love ourselves. Yet consider his character, and where is either goodness or greatness? He betrays Ophelia's gentlest love; he repulses her in a cruel manner; and when in the most touching way, she speaks to him, and returns his presents, he laughs her off like a man of the town. At her grave, at the new-made grave of Ophelia his first love, whom his own unkindness had blasted in the very bud of her beauty, in the morn and liquid dew of youth, what is the behaviour of Hamlet? A blank—worse than a blank; a few ranting lines, instead of true feeling, that prove him perfectly heartless. Then his behaviour in the grave, and his insult to Laertes, why the gentlest verdict one can give is insanity. But he seems by nature, and in his soberest moods, fiend-like in cruelty. His old companions Rosencrantz and Guildenstern, he murders without the least compunction; he desires them to be put to sudden death, "not

5. *Paradise Lost*, II, 146–148. The last line should read "Those thoughts."

shriving-time allowed." And the same diabolical refinement of revenge, when he finds the King at his prayers, induces him to wait for some more horrid time, "when he is drunk, asleep, or in his rage," to assassinate him, that "his soul may be as damned and black as hell, whereto he goes." Polonius, the father of Ophelia, he does actually kill; and for this does he lament or atone for what he has done, by any regret or remorse? "I'll lug the guts into the neighbour room."—"You shall nose him as you go up the stairs into the lobby!"

But suppose him heartless, though he is for ever lamenting, and complaining, and declaiming about the false-heartedness of every one else; Richard is heartless—Iago—Edmund. The tragic poet of course deals not in your good-boy characters. But neither is he, as Richard is, a hero, a man of mighty strength of mind. He is, according to his own admission, as "unlike Hercules" as possible. He does not, as a great and energetic mind does, exult under the greatness of a grand object. He is weak; so miserably weak as even to complain of his own weakness. He says

> The time is out of joint,—O cruel spite,
> That ever I was born to set it right.

And yet he is always boasting and bragging of his own powers, and scorning every one else, and he swears he will sweep to his revenge, "with wings as swift as meditation or the thoughts of love." For revenge was his love. But in truth he loved it, Shelley, after your own heart, most platonically; for his heart is too faint to win it fairly, and he contents himself with laughing at himself, mocking his own conscious cowardice, and venting his spleen in names, instead of doing any thing like a man. So irresolute is he, that he envies the players, he envies Fortinbras, Laertes, any one that can do any thing. Weak, irresolute, a talking sophist. Yet—O I am sick of this most lame and impotent hero?

Shelley. And yet we recognize in him something that we cannot but love and sympathise with, and a grandeur of tone which we instinctively reverence.

Byron. Then Ophelia, how gross are the scenes of her madness! She, too, seems as inconsistent and as false a character as her faithless lover. The graceful and gentle Ophelia changes somehow or other as shapes change in a dream, into an insane gypsy, singing no very delicate songs. Laertes is a braggadocio kind of fellow, and as for the rest of them, King and Queen, and Polonius:—why do we, through five long acts, interest ourselves in the fates and fortunes of such pitiful beings?

Shelley. But do you not admire the buried majesty of Denmark "revisiting the glimpses of the moon"?

"Alas! poor ghost!" said Byron. "I had forgot it, but the ghost is as whimsical a person as any of the others. It seems to come and go without any reason at all. Why should it make all that bustle in the cellarage when it cries out 'Swear!' in echo to Hamlet? Why should it appear so unexpectedly and uselessly in that scene with his mother? But ask not why, seek not reason, or consistency, or art, in the wild rhapsodies of this uncultivated genius."

Shelley. Are you then so orthodox in any thing as to think Shakespeare a man of no art or thought—a prophet of poetry, possessed by a spirit unintelligible to himself?

Byron. My dear fellow, who can read this very play, and call Shakespeare a thoughtful artist? Let us rise a little higher, and consider the whole play, and the play as a whole. The story, the action, after the first prologue and preparation of this ghost, remains stagnant; all the rest is stationary, episodical, useless. What is Fortinbras to the usurpation of the King, or the revenge of Hamlet, or any part of the plot? nor do Ophelia or Polonius conduce to the main of the story, or to the progress of the interest. Add a sufficient quantity [*quantum suff.*] of courtiers, players, grave-diggers, clowns, and such like stuff, ridiculous and incongruous, and out of all keeping with the high-heeled, tragic strut; useless, in truth, in relation to the play considered in itself; but I suppose poor Will found sufficient use and reason in the pence and praises of the gods of the galleries. And thus this will-o'the-wisp, this meteor of genius, leads us poor mortals, who would fain analyze his nature and detect his "airy purposes," a weary and a fruitless chase; while the simpler solution of the difficulty would be, that Shakespeare was a man of great genius but no art, and much preferred satisfying his hostess of the Mermaid with a good night's profit, to satisfying the troublesome and inquisitive readers of future ages, which he dreamed not of.

This seemed to make Shelley melancholy, and we walked in silence through the arched gateway into the public road; nothing was heard but the echo of our steps. I felt a kind of sorrow and mournful shame, as if the glory of man was proved indeed to be the "dream of a shadow." "But," said Shelley, beginning again, with the kind of wedgelike, thin voice with which a man brings in a solid argument that he is sure of, "What do you exactly mean by a great genius without art? do you mean a man who throws out in his writings some odd passages of great beauty, but leaves the whole, as a whole, rude and unformed?"

Byron. Take it that way, if you will.

Shelley. Well then, what do we mean by a beautiful passage or line? Is not a line, as well as your outspread heroics, or a tragedy, a whole, and only as a whole, beautiful in itself? as, for instance, "How sweet the moonlight sleeps upon this bank." Now, examining this line, we perceive that all the parts are formed in relation to one another, and that it is consequently a whole. "Sleep," we see, is a reduplication of the pure and gentle sound of sweet; and as the beginning of the former symphonizes with the beginning *s* of the latter, so also the *l* in moonlight prepares one for the *l* in sleep, and glides gently into it; and in the conclusion, one may perceive that the word "bank" is determined by the preceding words, and that the *b* which it begins with is but a deeper intonation of the two *p*'s which come before it; sleeps upon this slope, would have been effeminate; sleeps upon this rise, would have been harsh and inharmonious.

Byron. Heavens! do you imagine, my dear Shelley, that Shakespeare had any thing of the kind in his head when he struck off that pretty line? If any one had told him all this about your *p*'s and *s*'s, he would just have said, "Pish!"

Shelley. Well, be that as it may, are there not the coincidences, I suppose you would call them, that I showed in the line?

Byron. There are. But the beauty of the line does not lie in sounds and syllables, and such mechanical contrivances, but in the beautiful metaphor of the moonlight sleeping.

Shelley. Indeed, that also is very beautiful. In every single line, the poet must organize many simultaneous operations, both the meaning of the words and their emphatic arrangement, and then the flow and melting together of their symphony; and the whole must also be united with the current of the rhythm.

Byron. Well, then, I'm glad I'm not a poet! It must be like making out one's expenses for a journey, I think, all this calculation!

Shelley. I don't say that a poet must necessarily be conscious of all this, no more than a lady is conscious of every graceful movement. But I do say that they all depend upon reason, in which they live and move, and have their being; and that he who brings them out into the light of distinct consciousness, beside satisfying an instinctive desire of his own nature, will be more secure and more commanding. But what makes this metaphor beautiful? To represent the tranquillity of moonlight is the object of the line; and the sleep is beautiful, because it gives a more intense and living form of the same idea; the rhythm beautifully falls in with this, and just lets the cadence of the emphasis dwell upon the sound and sense of the sweet word "sleep"; and the alliteration assimilates the rest of the line into one harmonious symmetry. This line, therefore, is it not altogether a work of art?

Byron. If it is, I don't see what this has to do with the discussion about Hamlet.

Shelley. Why, just this. You recollect, you said Shakespeare was a great genius with no art?

Byron. Yes.

Shelley. And that you meant by that, a man who would strike out two or three good lines, and purple patches of poetry in his work, but who leaves the whole unfinished?

Byron. Yes.

Shelley. And we afterwards agreed that every line, or part of a line, that was good, was made good by art only?

Byron. Well!

Shelley. Why, then, this is the conclusion, that a man of great genius, but little art, means only, one who is able to perceive in the small what his powers are not wide enough to comprehend in the greater.

Byron. Well, well—for heaven's sake, what does it signify about the *words*, art, or genius? This does not explain Hamlet.

Shelley. Only that, if what I have said is true, and if Shakespeare is one of the most glorious names among mankind, and Hamlet one of his most famous plays, it is more than probable that he was not so blind as you would make him; and that there must be some point of view, if we could find it, some proper distance and happy light, in which the whole would appear a beautiful whole. I once attempted a kind of commentary upon this very play, and if you will allow me, I will read it to you.

Byron, though half provoked and half amused, with what he thought the mad and ridiculous speculations and imaginations of his friend, agreed—and, after dinner, Shelley read us out his view of Hamlet:—

"The character of Hamlet himself we must first endeavour to penetrate into, and if we can understand this central germ, we shall be better able to follow the poet in the conception and organization of his great work, and to see how every part is what it is necessarily, and bears in itself the reason of its existence and its form.

"The character of Hamlet, as I take it, represents the profound philosopher; or, rather, the errors to which a contemplative and ideal mind is liable: for of necessity the lessons of the tragic poet are like the demonstrations, *ex absurdo*, of Parmenides, since the mind's eye is so dull and blinded, so 'drunk-asleep,' to use Hamlet's words, as not by intuition to recognize the beauty of virtue, to prove it, as it were, by the clashing contradiction of the two opposite extremes: as, if a man derived a more sensible, or rather sensual, consciousness of health, which also is indeed a gift of the same Apollo who bestows upon us truth and beauty, from having been previously in sickness: —there is but one demonstration of the excellence of health, and that is disease.

"Purposing, therefore, to body forth a character so deeply, indeed, and pre-eminently tragic, but most hard to fix and bring down into the definite world of action, as it seemed to lie beyond it in the sphere of thought, silent and invisible, Shakespeare invented the sublime idea of the ghost; an outward and visible sign of the sudden apparitions of the mysterious world within us. The ghost of his father, clad in complete steel, revisiting the glimpses of the moon, may be considered as a great purpose coming suddenly upon a meditative mind.

All the outward circumstance and actual reality, of course, immediately become necessary as the laws and conditions of the visible world into which it is translated. Now Hamlet the father was a man of action: his character is finely realized for us in two admirable lines, where, describing the appearance of this buried majesty, Marcellus says—

> So frown'd he once, when in an angry parle
> He smote the sledded Polack on the ice.

But his son Hamlet, brooding over the remembrance of his father, has embarked upon that shoreless sea of melancholy,

> Whose bottom none could ever sound, or find
> The ooze, to show what coast his sluggish craft
> Might easiliest harbour in.

At the time when the play opens, he is about thirty years old, as we learn from the clown in the fifth act. He is by birth a German; and from indulging in the inactive habits of that deep-thinking nation, he has become 'fat, and scant of breath,' as the Queen says. He has passed all his life at Wittenberg, famous in Shakespeare's time, as the college of Dr. Faustus; and we know that he had there been very much with the players. At the court, he still lived a recluse life, complaining of the excesses of the times, and 'walking for hours in the lobby' reading or meditating.

"The play opens with mysterious notes of preparation,—

> And prologues to the omen'd coming-on.

We are far removed from all the stir of society, in the solitude of the open air and darkness; only distant noises from the palace come at intervals, making solitude more solitary; the soldiers of the watch begin talking mysteriously about the signs of the times, 'dreaming on things to come,' when the ghost appears. In the next scene, we come back into the pomp and pride of the world, and kings and courtiers: Hamlet is among them, but not of them. His very first words are most significant of his character, when he exclaims, 'Seems, Madam! I know not seems.' Observe, too, when Horatio tells him of this wonderful appearance, how philosophical his questions are, as of a man trying to realize completely, in his own mind, the image of the thing. The mysterious contradiction between reality and ideality, one of the most profound questions of ontology, is strongly shown in the beginning of this dialogue. 'My father! methinks I see my father!' —'O where, my Lord?' cries Horatio, starting in terror. 'In my mind's eye, Horatio.' To this subject Hamlet recurs again, in the conversation with his two good friends: 'There is,' says he, 'nothing either good or bad, but thinking makes it so.' And again in another place, where Osric asks 'if he knows Laertes?' he replies, 'I dare not confess that, lest I should compare with him in excellence; for to know a man well were to know oneself.'

"In the next scene of the first act, Hamlet, in the midst of a long metaphysical speculation, in which he had forgot all time and place, is suddenly visited by the apparition. He breaks off in terror. When the ghost has faded from him, he is left overcome with his feelings, and with the weight of the commanded action. He confuses his external body with his inner self, as if he were nothing but a spirit; and when he says that he will raze out all that he learned from experience or from thought,

> And thy commandment all alone shall live
> Within the book and volume of my brain,

he takes out his real tablets and writes it down.

"The levity of his expressions afterwards is most true to nature; and the mysterious movements of the ghost make flesh and blood shudder to think upon the invisible world that is around us, and within us, and whose purposes, and silent operations and recoilings, are to us most awfully unaccountable.

"But the great artist, between these two more intense scenes, has interposed a gentler shade, which not only relieves and alleviates the deeper interests of the tragedy, but brings out also many new views of Hamlet's character, and marks the moral of the whole more deeply. She was a beautiful young creature,

> Forward, not permanent; sweet, not lasting,

but not the woman to fix or seriously engage the mighty mind of Hamlet; and thus he is here also perplexed with the difference between mind and body; and she, like a dew-drop from a lion's mane, is shaken to air. As to old politic Polonius, his precepts are most amusing; certainly they are the very reverse of Hamlet's ignorance of all external seemings, as they appear to know nothing but appearances, and they all follow each other, after the manner of his own sage simile, 'as the night the day,' that is, without any method of reason.

"The whole play is a play of plots and contrivances of all sorts, and an endless extravagance of ingenuity in every thing; and the first scene of this act shows us Polonius, who is a kind of mock Hamlet, or a Hamlet grown old, and with nothing left of 'the soul of wit' but the husk and 'frothing circumstance,' the limbs and outward flourishes—and here we see him working at his little under-plots with windlasses and with assays of bias—

By indirections to find directions out.

Hamlet, meanwhile, in pursuance of his plan of pretending madness, which, indeed, he does by indulging into excess his own real feelings, and thus feeding the loneliness of his heart with exaggerated solitude; led now by the instinct of his shock at the detected infamy of his mother, has frightened poor Ophelia, and so set off all these sage old folk—

Who hunt the trail of policy so sure—

on the very scent which he intended; where let us leave them in full sonorous cry.

"The next scenes are too insignificant to require any comment, excepting, perhaps, Hamlet's letter. Many have agreed with Polonius in thinking 'beautified' a vile phrase; but it is just of a piece with his signature,—'while this machine is to him, Hamlet,'—and only shows in every thing his metaphysical turn of thought. 'My soul's idol' sounds ordinary, but Hamlet, I do not doubt, meant it more accurately.

"Rosencrantz and Guildenstern, as Goethe well observes, are a brace of those half creatures, who, taken single, would be nothing, and always take care to go in couples. How deplorable would the smiling but crooked-councilling Rosencrantz have been without the

guilded and guileful Guildenstern! But here come men much more
to Hamlet's taste—how heartily he welcomes them!—there are the
players. The introduction of these players is one of the most admirable and artful inventions of any in all Shakespeare. They represent
the whole body of literature, 'whose object is, and always has been,'
as Hamlet with his usual profundity observes, 'to hold up the
mirror to nature,' and is dedicated to the same light-giving God who
bestows upon us the heaven-descended know thyself [γνωθι σεαυτον].
We have here an opportunity of learning something of Hamlet's
taste, and we accordingly find him deeply delighted with the most
lofty and imaginative poetry that ever swept over a theatre in tragic
pall.

"The verses themselves, as that most excellent critic Schlegel
observes, are necessarily elevated two degrees above nature to
modesty of nature, that they might stand out from the rest, as a
play within a play. They seem like a thing seen through a magnifying glass; and are, indeed, one of the most extraordinary productions
of wondrous Shakespearian art. Hamlet's soliloquy, which crowns
and concludes the act, is not merely the casual product of a chance
situation, but, like every work of Shakespeare's mind, contains or
implies a profound view of some important question—in the present
case the relative situations of the two loftiest divisions of human
intellect—the poet's and the philosopher's. In his next soliloquy,
the famous 'To be or not to be,' we may observe developed, in a
grand style, the peculiarity of Hamlet's mind, its tendency to
idealize every thing; he quite forgets the reality of the case, and
impersonates in one all the ills that flesh is heir to—

The pangs of despised love, the law's delay, &c.

"And this we must bear in mind against the scene at Ophelia's
grave, for Hamlet was not selfish.

"But he was disposed to idealize to excess. What a deep feeling
both of his weakness, and yet the grandeur of his strength is conveyed
in his address to his friend—

Horatio, thou art e'en as *just* a man,
As e'er my conversation cop'd withal.

"After the play, he is much in the same state of uncertainty and vacillation in which the ghost left him; he recoils and swerves from action; and it is an instinctive feeling of this sort that makes him impatient even of the necessities of versification,—any thing necessary he feels a disposition to resist or avoid.

> For thou dost know, O Damon dear,
> This realm dismantled was
> Of Jove himself, and now reigns here,
> A very, very—peacock.

"'You might have rhymed,' says the man of just sense, Horatio. But there is the same lame and impotent conclusion in every thing he does. Soon after this, when he tries to lash himself into exertion, reminding himself of the ghostly time of night, and graves giving up their dead, and vaunting as extravagantly as falsely, 'Now could I drink hot blood,' &c. his considerations about killing his mother, and determinations *not* to do it, are but a bitter though unconscious mockery of himself, and just an antistrophe to his curious refinements on the murder of the king. In both cases it is but the excess of an over ingenious intellect,

> With thinking too precisely on the event.

"There is a deep meaning signified in the next scene with his mother, where, in the midst of his declamation, gazing upon the picture, the reality suddenly comes. Always his profound meditations seem without beginning or end, while he wanders in a wilderness of thought, and enterprises of great moment, while he is declaiming with the player, or tracing the dust of imperial Cæsar to a bunghole, or flattering his own weakness with proving to himself the shallowness of all the actions and the actors of life, become 'sicklied o'er with this pale cast, and lose the name of action.' Whenever he does any thing, he seems astonished at himself, and calls it rashness.

> Rashly, and praised be rashness for it—

as he tells his friend Horatio, he set about his deliverance from the false ambassadors. In the next lines he gives, in my opinion, the moral of the whole:

Let us know
There's a divinity that shapes our ends,
Rough hew them how we will.

"'That is most certain,' Horatio replies.

"How different is Laertes. *His* father also has been murdered—but he at once collects the people, storms the palace, compels the king, at his peril, to account for the murder. Nothing, he cries, shall stop him, but 'my will, not all the world's.' His will he follows impetuously; he looks not to right or left, with 'considering too curiously.' But he errs on the other side. He raises the mob—he would, he says, of Hamlet, 'cut his throat in church.' He does kill him with a treacherous poisoned rapier. His thoughts are so fixed upon his end, that he sees not any thing between.

"Now such a rash gunpowder spark as this Laertes, Hamlet must at once have envied and despised. Well, they meet at the grave of Ophelia—for the simple young creature, half by accident, and half on purpose, in her half-witted state, drowned herself. The simplicity of her girlish youthfulness, and the manner in which Hamlet had wooed her, became sufficiently evident in her ballads; her character was necessarily what it is—for in a play so full of thought, and the deepest interests of the soul, a more strong passion would have been a note, 'harsh, and of dissonant mood.'

"Hamlet, when he discovers her death, only says, 'What! the fair Ophelia!' But when this Laertes, who always so outran his thoughts with an excess of hair-brained action, leaps into the grave, and declaims 'with such an emphasis and phrase of sorrow,' Hamlet is thrown into a towering passion, and conscious of the weakness and vagueness of his own feelings on the occasion, he cries out, in the bitterness of his contempt, both for Laertes and himself

—Show me what thou 'lt do!
Woul't weep, woul't fight, woul't fast, woul't tear thyself,
Woul't drink up esel? eat a crocodile?

"What falseness is all this sorrow of yours!—I could do just as much, Come, what shall we do?—weep, or fast, or tear our hair, or drink vinegar, or eat crocodiles to make ourselves shed false tears! &c. But Hamlet is ever a perfect gentleman, and his apology to

Laertes is one of those gentle mellowings and softenings of a strong outline which Shakespeare so well understood. With regard to his alleged cruelty, this appearance arose from his philosophical habit of seeing every thing as laws, or necessary consequences.

"As Spinoza says of himself, 'humanas actiones non ridere, non lugere, neque detestari, sed intelligere'—'neither to laugh at, or bewail, or detest the actions of men; but to understand them.' He allowed the two false courtiers no shriving time, because it was necessary for his plot—if they should be heard, all would be found out—and he says, 'They come not near my conscience,' viewing it as a general and necessary case.

> 'Tis dangerous when the baser nature comes,
> Between the pass and fell incensed points
> Of mighty opposites.

"What noble lines! But we have passed a hundred admirable and significant groups and views; we have missed the clown and the gravedigger. In Shakespeare 'one may suck matter out of every thing, as a weasel sucks eggs,' as Jacques says. These clowns are very like their betters, they are not thinking of the thing they are about; but make themselves happy in the exercise of an endless ingenuity.

"Fortinbras shuts the scene. He surrounds the play as with a frame.

"It appears, therefore, that Hamlet is, in itself, a complete and reasonable whole, composed in an harmonious proportion of difference and similitude, into one expressive unity."

Shelley, as he finished, looked up, and found Lord Byron fast asleep.

"Byron and Shelley on the Character of Hamlet," *New Monthly Magazine and Literary Journal*, N.S. XXIX (1830), pt. ii, 327–336.

Appendix B
Thomas Love Peacock's
"The Four Ages of Poetry"

Thomas Love Peacock (1785–1866), poet and writer of satiric novels, first became acquainted with Shelley in 1812. Though not a university man, Peacock shared with Shelley a deep interest in Greek. While Shelley lived in England, the two were often together, and later they corresponded often. Peacock's practical and conservative tastes led him to disapprove many of Shelley's ideas, but the friendship was unbroken until Shelley's death. In 1858, 1860, and 1862 Peacock contributed memoirs of Shelley to Fraser's Magazine *which were later published as* Memorials of Shelley *(1909).*

Peacock contributed "The Four Ages of Poetry" to the first number of Ollier's Literary Miscellany *in 1820. Satiric in intention, the essay nevertheless is in part a serious rejection of tendencies in English poetry of the period. Peacock may have intended to draw Shelley out. Shelley's first comment was to the publishers, whom he knew well: "It is very clever, but, I think, very false." In this letter of January 20, 1821, Shelley states his intention to write a reply, and offers to send it for a future number of the* Miscellany. *As it turned out, the* Miscellany *was discontinued after the first number.*

Those who feed on these things can have no more taste than those who live in the kitchen can be in good odor.—Petronius.[1]

Poetry, like the world, may be said to have four ages, but in a different order: the first age of poetry being the age of iron; the second, of gold; the third of silver; and the fourth of brass.

The first, or iron age of poetry, is that in which rude bards

1. "*Qui inter haec nutriuntur non magis sapere possunt, quam bene olere qui in culinâ habitant.*"

celebrate in rough numbers the exploits of ruder chiefs, in days when every man is a warrior, and when the great practical maxim of every form of society, "to keep what we have and to catch what we can," is not yet disguised under names of justice and forms of law, but is the naked motto of the naked sword, which is the only judge and jury in every question of mine and thine [*meum* and *tuum*]. In these days, the only three trades flourishing (besides that of priest, which flourishes always) are those of king, thief, and beggar: the beggar being, for the most part, a king deject, and the thief a king expectant. The first question asked of a stranger is, whether he is a beggar or a thief:[2] the stranger, in reply, usually assumes the first, and awaits a convenient opportunity to prove his claim to the second appellation.

The natural desire of every man to engross to himself as much power and property as he can acquire by any of the means which might makes right, is accompanied by the no less natural desire of making known to as many people as possible the extent to which he has been a winner in this universal game. The successful warrior becomes a chief; the successful chief becomes a king: his next want is an organ to disseminate the fame of his achievements and the extent of his possessions; and this organ he finds in a bard, who is always ready to celebrate the strength of his arm, being first duly inspired by that of his liquor. This is the origin of poetry, which, like all other trades, takes its rise in the demand for the commodity, and flourishes in proportion to the extent of the market.

Poetry is thus in its origin panegyrical. The first rude songs of all nations appear to be a sort of brief historical notices, in a strain of tumid hyperbole, of the exploits and possessions of a few pre-eminent individuals. They tell us how many battles such an one has fought, how many helmets he has cleft, how many breastplates he has pierced, how many widows he has made, how much land he has appropriated, how many houses he has demolished for other people, what a large one he has built for himself, how much gold he has stowed away in it, and how liberally and plentifully he pays, feeds, and intoxicates the divine and immortal bards, the sons of Jupiter, but for whose everlasting songs the names of heroes would perish.

2. See the Odyssey, *passim*: and Thucydides, I, 5. [Peacock's note.]

This is the first stage of poetry before the invention of written letters. The numerical modulation is at once useful as a help to memory, and pleasant to the ears of uncultured men, who are easily caught by sound: and, from the exceeding flexibility of the yet unformed language, the poet does no violence to his ideas in subjecting them to the fetters of number. The savage, indeed, lisps in numbers, and all rude and uncivilized people express themselves in the manner which we call poetical.

The scenery by which he is surrounded, and the superstitions which are the creed of his age, form the poet's mind. Rocks, mountains, seas, unsubdued forests, unnavigable rivers, surround him with forms of power and mystery, which ignorance and fear have peopled with spirits, under multifarious names of gods, goddesses, nymphs, genii, and dæmons. Of all these personages marvellous tales are in existence: the nymphs are not indifferent to handsome young men, and the gentlemen-genii are much troubled and very troublesome with a propensity to be rude to pretty maidens: the bard, therefore, finds no difficulty in tracing the genealogy of his chief to any of the deities in his neighbourhood with whom the said chief may be most desirous of claiming relationship.

In this pursuit, as in all others, some, of course, will attain a very marked pre-eminence; and these will be held in high honour, like Demodocus in the Odyssey, and will be consequently inflated with boundless vanity, like Thamyris in the Iliad. Poets are as yet the only historians and chroniclers of their time, and the sole depositories of all the knowledge of their age; and though this knowledge is rather a crude congeries of traditional phantasies than a collection of useful truths, yet, such as it is, they have it to themselves. They are observing and thinking, while others are robbing and fighting: and though their object be nothing more than to secure a share of the spoil, yet they accomplish this end by intellectual, not by physical power: their success excites emulation to the attainment of intellectual eminence: thus they sharpen their own wits and awaken those of others, at the same time that they gratify vanity and amuse curiosity. A skilful display of the little knowledge they have gains them credit for the possession of much more which they have not. Their familiarity with the secret history of gods and genii obtains for them, without much difficulty, the reputation of inspiration; thus they are not only historians, but theologians, moralists, and legislators: delivering their oracles *ex cathedrâ*, and being indeed often themselves (as Orpheus and Amphion) regarded as portions and emanations of divinity: building cities with a song, and leading brutes with a symphony; which are only metaphors for the faculty of leading multitudes by the nose.

The golden age of poetry finds its materials in the age of iron. This age begins when poetry begins to be retrospective; when something like a more extended system of civil polity is established; when personal strength and courage avail less to the aggrandizing of their possessor, and to the making and marring of kings and kingdoms, and are checked by organized bodies, social institutions, and hereditary successions. Men also live more in the light of truth and within the interchange of observation; and thus perceive that the agency of gods and genii is not so frequent among themselves as, to judge from the songs and legends of the past time, it was among their ancestors. From these two circumstances, really diminished personal power, and apparently diminished familiarity with gods and genii, they very easily and naturally deduce two conclusions: 1st, That men are degenerated, and 2nd, That they are less in favour with the gods. The people of the petty states and colonies, which have now acquired stability and form, which owed their origin and first prosperity to the talents and courage of a single chief, magnify their founder through the mists of distance and tradition, and perceive him achieving wonders with a god or goddess always at his elbow. They find his name and his exploits thus magnified and accompanied in their traditionary songs, which are their only memorials. All that is said of him is in this character. There is nothing to contradict it. The man and his exploits and his tutelary deities are mixed and blended in one invariable association. The marvellous, too, is very much like a snow-ball: it grows as it rolls downward, till the little nucleus of truth, which began its descent from the summit, is hidden in the accumulation of superinduced hyperbole.

When tradition, thus adorned and exaggerated, has surrounded the founders of families and states with so much adventitious power and magnificence, there is no praise which a living poet can, without fear of being kicked for clumsy flattery, address to a living chief, that will not still leave the impression that the latter is not so great a man as his ancestors. The man must, in this case, be praised through his ancestors. Their greatness must be established, and he must be shown to be their worthy descendant. All the people of a state are interested in the founder of their state. All states that have harmonized into a common form of society, are interested in their respective founders. All men are interested in their ancestors. All men love to look back into the days that are past. In these circumstances traditional national poetry is reconstructed and brought, like chaos, into order and form. The interest is more universal: understanding is enlarged: passion still has scope and play: character is still various and strong: nature is still unsubdued and existing in all her beauty and magnificence, and men are not yet excluded from her observation by the magnitude of cities, or the daily confinement of civic life: poetry is more an art: it requires greater skill in numbers, greater command of language, more extensive and various knowledge, and greater comprehensiveness of mind. It still exists without rivals in any other department of literature; and even the arts, painting and sculpture certainly, and music probably, are comparatively rude and imperfect. The whole field of intellect is its own. It has no rivals in history, nor in philosophy, nor in science. It is cultivated by the greatest intellects of the age, and listened to by all the rest. This is the age of Homer, the golden age of poetry. Poetry has now attained its perfection: it has attained the point which it cannot pass: genius therefore seeks new forms for the treatment of the same subjects: hence the lyric poetry of Pindar and Alcæus, and the tragic poetry of Æschylus and Sophocles. The favour of kings, the honour of the Olympic crown, the applause of present multitudes, all that can feed vanity and stimulate rivalry, await the successful cultivator of this art, till its forms become exhausted, and new rivals arise around it in new fields of literature, which gradually acquire more influence as, with the progress of reason and civilization, facts become more interesting than fiction: indeed, the maturity of poetry may be considered the infancy of history. The transition from Homer to Herodotus is scarcely more remarkable than that from Herodotus to Thucydides in the gradual dereliction of fabulous incident and ornamented language. Herodotus is as much a poet in relation to Thucydides as Homer is in relation to Herodotus. The history of Herodotus is half a poem: it was written while the whole field of literature yet belonged to the Muses, and the nine books of which it was composed were therefore of right, as well as of courtesy, superinscribed with their nine names.

Speculations, too, and disputes, on the nature of man and of mind; on moral duties and on good and evil; on the animate and inanimate components of the visible world; begin to share attention with the eggs of Leda and the horns of Io, and to draw off from poetry a portion of its once undivided audience.

Then comes the silver age, or the poetry of civilized life. This poetry is of two kinds, imitative and original. The imitative consists in recasting, and giving an exquisite polish to the poetry of the age of gold: of this Virgil is the most obvious and striking example. The original is chiefly comic, didactic, or satiric: as in Menander, Aristophanes, Horace, and Juvenal. The poetry of this age is characterized by an exquisite and fastidious selection of words, and a laboured and somewhat monotonous harmony of expression: but its monotony consists in this, that experience having exhausted all the varieties of modulation, the civilized poetry selects the most beautiful, and prefers the repetition of these to ranging through the variety of all. But the best expression being that into which the idea naturally falls, it requires the utmost labour and care so to reconcile the inflexibility of civilized language and the laboured polish of versification with the idea intended to be expressed, that sense may not appear to be sacrificed to sound. Hence numerous efforts and rare success.

This state of poetry is, however, a step towards its extinction. Feeling and passion are best painted in, and roused by, ornamental and figurative language; but the reason and the understanding are best addressed in the simplest and most unvarnished phrase. Pure reason and dispassionate truth would be perfectly ridiculous in verse, as we may judge by versifying one of Euclid's demonstrations. This will be found true of all dispassionate reasoning whatever, and of all reasoning that requires comprehensive views and enlarged combinations. It is only the more tangible points of morality, those which command assent at once, those which have a mirror in every mind, and in which the severity of reason is warmed and rendered palatable by being mixed up with feeling and imagination, that are applicable even to what is called moral poetry: and as the sciences of morals and of mind advance towards perfection, as they become more enlarged and comprehensive in their views, as reason gains the ascendancy in them over imagination and feeling, poetry can no longer accompany them in their progress, but drops into the background, and leaves them to advance alone.

Thus the empire of thought is withdrawn from poetry, as the empire of facts had been before. In respect of the latter, the poet of the age of iron celebrates the achievements of his contemporaries; the poet of the age of gold celebrates the heroes of the age of iron; the poet of the age of silver re-casts the poems of the age of gold: we may here see how very slight a ray of historical truth is sufficient to dissipate all the illusions of poetry. We know no more of the men than of the gods of the Iliad; no more of Achilles than we do of Thetis; no more of Hector and Andromache than we do of Vulcan and Venus: these belong altogether to poetry; history has no share in them: but Virgil knew better than to write an epic about Cæsar; he left him to Livy; and travelled out of the confines of truth and history into the old regions of poetry and fiction.

Good sense and elegant learning, conveyed in polished and somewhat monotonous verse, are the perfection of the original and imitative poetry of civilized life. Its range is limited, and when exhausted, nothing remains but the warmed-over cabbage [*crambe repetita*] of commonplace, which at length becomes thoroughly wearisome, even to the most indefatigable readers of the newest new nothings.

It is now evident that poetry must either cease to be cultivated, or strike into a new path. The poets of the age of gold have been imitated and repeated till no new imitation will attract notice: the limited range of ethical and didactic poetry is exhausted: the associations of daily life in an advanced state of society are of very dry, methodical, unpoetical matters-of-fact: but there is always a multitude of listless idlers, yawning for amusement, and gaping for novelty: and the poet makes it his glory to be foremost among their purveyors.

Then comes the age of brass, which, by rejecting the polish and the learning of the age of silver, and taking a retrograde stride to the barbarisms and crude traditions of the age of iron, professes to return to nature and revive the age of gold. This is the second childhood of poetry. To the comprehensive energy of the Homeric Muse, which, by giving at once the grand outline of things, presented to the mind a vivid picture in one or two verses, inimitable alike in simplicity and magnificence, is substituted a verbose and minutely-detailed description of thoughts, passions, actions, persons, and things, in that loose rambling style of verse, which any one may write, standing on one foot [*stans pede in uno*], at the rate of two hundred lines in an hour. To this age may be referred all the poets who flourished in the decline of the Roman Empire. The best specimen of it, though not the most generally known, is the Dionysiaca of Nonnus, which contains many passages of exceeding beauty in the midst of masses of amplification and repetition.

The iron age of classical poetry may be called the bardic; the golden, the Homeric; the silver, the Virgilian; and the brass, the Nonnic.

Modern poetry has also its four ages: but "it wears its rue with a difference."

To the age of brass in the ancient world succeeded the dark ages, in which the light of the Gospel began to spread over Europe, and in which, by a mysterious and inscrutable dispensation, the darkness thickened with the progress of the light. The tribes that overran the Roman Empire brought back the days of barbarism, but with this difference, that there were many books in the world, many places in which they were preserved, and occasionally some one by whom they were read, who indeed (if he escaped being burned *pour l'amour de Dieu*) generally lived an object of mysterious fear, with the reputation of magician, alchymist, and astrologer. The emerging of the nations of Europe from this superinduced barbarism, and their settling into new forms of polity, was accompanied, as the first ages of Greece had been, with a wild spirit of adventure, which, co-operating with new manners and new superstitions, raised up a fresh crop of chimæras, not less fruitful, though far less beautiful, than those of Greece. The semi-deification of women by the maxims of the age of chivalry, combining with these new fables, produced the romance of the middle ages. The founders of the new line of heroes took the place of the demi-gods of Grecian poetry. Charlemagne and his Paladins, Arthur and his knights of the round table, the heroes of the iron age of chivalrous poetry, were seen through the same magnifying mist of distance, and their exploits were celebrated with even more extravagant hyperbole. These legends, combined with the exaggerated love that pervades the songs of the troubadours, the reputation of magic that attached to learned men, the infant wonders of natural philosophy, the crazy fanaticism of the crusades, the power and privileges of the great feudal chiefs, and the holy mysteries of monks and nuns, formed a state of society in which no two laymen could meet without fighting, and in which the three staple ingredients of lover, prize-fighter, and fanatic, that composed the basis of the character of every true man, were mixed up and diversified, in different individuals and classes, with so many distinctive excellences, and under such an infinite motley variety of costume, as gave the range of a most extensive and picturesque field to the two great constituents of poetry, love and battle.

From these ingredients of the iron age of modern poetry, dispersed in the rhymes of ministrels and the songs of the troubadours, arose the golden age, in which the scattered materials were harmonized and blended about the time of the revival of learning; but with this peculiar difference, that Greek and Roman literature pervaded all the poetry of the golden age of modern poetry, and hence resulted a heterogeneous compound of all ages and nations in one picture; an infinite licence, which gave to the poet the free range of the whole field of imagination and memory. This was carried very far by Ariosto, but farthest of all by Shakespeare and his contemporaries, who used time and locality merely because they could not do without them, because every action must have its when and where: but they made no scruple of deposing a Roman Emperor by an Italian Count, and sending him off in the disguise of a French pilgrim to be shot with a blunderbuss by an English archer. This makes the old English drama very picturesque, at any rate, in the variety of costume, and very diversified in action and character; though it is a picture of nothing that ever was seen on earth except a Venetian carnival.

The greatest of English poets, Milton, may be said to stand alone between the ages of gold and silver, combining the excellences of both; for with all the energy, and power, and freshness of the first, he united all the studied and elaborate magnificence of the second.

The silver age succeeded; beginning with Dryden, coming to perfection with Pope, and ending with Goldsmith, Collins, and Gray.

Cowper divested verse of its exquisite polish; he thought in metre, but paid more attention to his thoughts than his verse. It would be difficult to draw the boundary of prose and blank verse between his letters and his poetry.

The silver age was the reign of authority; but authority now began to be shaken, not only in poetry but in the whole sphere of its dominion. The contemporaries of Gray and Cowper were deep and elaborate thinkers. The subtle scepticism of Hume, the solemn irony of Gibbon, the daring paradoxes of Rousseau, and the biting ridicule of Voltaire, directed the energies of four extraordinary minds to shake every portion of the reign of authority. Inquiry was roused, the activity of intellect was excited, and poetry came in for its share of the general result. The changes had been rung on lovely maid and sylvan shade, summer heat and green retreat, waving trees and sighing breeze, gentle swains and amorous pains, by versifiers who took them on trust, as meaning something very soft and tender, without much caring what: but with this general activity of intellect came a necessity for even poets to appear to know something of what they professed to talk of. Thomson and Cowper looked at the trees and hills which so many ingenious gentlemen had rhymed about so long without looking at them at all, and the effect of the operation on poetry was like the discovery of a new world. Painting shared the influence, and the principles of picturesque beauty were explored by adventurous essayists with indefatigable pertinacity. The success which attended these experiments, and the pleasure which resulted from them, had the usual effect of all new enthusiasms, that of turning the heads of a few unfortunate persons, the patriarchs of the age of brass, who, mistaking the prominent novelty for the all-important totality, seem to have ratiocinated much in the following manner: "Poetical genius is the finest of all things, and we feel that we have more of it than any one ever had. The way to bring it to perfection is to cultivate poetical impressions exclusively. Poetical impressions can be received only among natural scenes: for all that is artificial is anti-poetical. Society is artificial, therefore we will live out of society. The mountains are natural, therefore we will live in the mountains. There we shall be shining models of purity and virtue, passing the whole day in the innocent and amiable occupation of going up and down hill, receiving poetical impressions, and communicating them in immortal verse to admiring generations." To some such perversion of intellect we owe that egregious confraternity of rhymesters, known by the name of the Lake Poets; who certainly did receive and communicate to the world some of the most extraordinary poetical impressions that ever were heard of, and ripened into models of public virtue, too splendid to need illustration. They wrote verses on a new principle; saw rocks and rivers in a new light; and remaining studiously ignorant of history, society, and human nature, cultivated the phantasy only at the expense of the memory and the reason; and contrived, though they had retreated from the world for the express purpose of seeing nature as she was, to see her only as she was not, converting the land they lived in into a sort of fairy-land, which they peopled with mysticisms and chimæras. This gave what is called a new tone to poetry, and conjured up a herd of desperate imitators, who have brought the age of brass prematurely to its dotage.

The descriptive poetry of the present day has been called by its cultivators a return to nature. Nothing is more impertinent than this pretension. Poetry cannot travel out of the regions of its birth, the uncultivated lands of semi-civilized men. Mr. Wordsworth, the great leader of the returners to nature, cannot describe a scene under his own eyes without putting into it the shadow of a Danish boy or the living ghost of Lucy Gray, or some similar phantastical parturition of the moods of his own mind.

In the origin and perfection of poetry, all the associations of life were composed of poetical materials. With us it is decidedly the reverse. We know too that there are no Dryads in Hyde-park nor Naiads in the Regent's-canal. But barbaric manners and supernatural interventions are essential to poetry. Either in the scene, or in the time, or in both, it must be remote from our ordinary perceptions. While the historian and the philosopher are advancing in, and accelerating, the progress of knowledge, the poet is wallowing in the rubbish of departed ignorance, and raking up the ashes of dead savages to find gewgaws and rattles for the grown babies of the age. Mr. Scott digs up the poachers and cattle-stealers of the ancient border. Lord Byron cruises for thieves and pirates on the shores of the Morea and among the Greek islands. Mr. Southey wades through ponderous volumes of travels and old chronicles, from which he carefully selects all that is false, useless, and absurd, as being essentially poetical; and when he has a commonplace book full of monstrosities, strings them into an epic. Mr. Wordsworth picks up village legends from old women and sextons; and Mr. Coleridge, to the valuable information acquired from similar sources, super-adds the dreams of crazy theologians and the mysticisms of German metaphysics, and favours the world with visions in verse, in which the quadruple elements of sexton, old woman, Jeremy Taylor, and Emanuel Kant are harmonized into a delicious poetical compound. Mr. Moore presents us with a Persian, and Mr. Campbell with a Pennsylvanian tale, both formed on the same principle as Mr. Southey's epics, by extracting from a perfunctory and desultory perusal of a collection of voyages and travels, all that useful investigation would not seek for and that common sense would reject.

These disjointed relics of tradition and fragments of second-hand observation, being woven into a tissue of verse, constructed on what Mr. Coleridge calls a new principle (that is, no principle at all), compose a modern-antique compound of frippery and barbarism, in which the puling sentimentality of the present time is grafted on the misrepresented ruggedness of the past into a heterogeneous congeries of unamalgamating manners, sufficient to impose on the common readers of poetry, over whose understandings the poet of this class possesses that commanding advantage, which, in all circumstances and conditions of life, a man who knows something, however little, always possesses over one who knows nothing.

A poet in our times is a semi-barbarian in a civilized community. He lives in the days that are past. His ideas, thoughts, feelings, associations, are all with barbarous manners, obsolete customs, and exploded superstitions. The march of his intellect is like that of a crab, backward. The brighter the light diffused around him by the progress of reason, the thicker is the darkness of antiquated barbarism, in which he buries himself like a mole, to throw up the barren hillocks of his Cimmerian labours. The philosophic mental tranquillity which looks round with an equal eye on all external things, collects a store of ideas, discriminates their relative value, assigns to all their proper place, and from the materials of useful knowledge thus collected, appreciated, and arranged, forms new combinations that impress the stamp of their power and utility on the real business of life, is diametrically the reverse of that frame of mind which poetry inspires, or from which poetry can emanate. The highest inspirations of poetry are resolvable into three ingredients: the rant of unregulated passion, the whining of exaggerated feeling, and the cant of factitious sentiment: and can therefore serve only to ripen a splendid lunatic like Alexander, a puling driveller like Werter, or a morbid dreamer like Wordsworth. It can never make a philosopher, nor a statesman, nor in any class of life an useful or rational man. It cannot claim the slightest share in any one of the comforts and utilities of life of which we have witnessed so many and so rapid advances. But though not useful, it may be said it is highly ornamental, and deserves to be cultivated for the pleasure it yields. Even if this be granted, it does not follow that a writer of poetry in the present state of society is not a waster of his own time, and a robber of that of others. Poetry is not one of those arts which, like painting, require repetition and multiplication, in order to be diffused among society. There are more good poems already existing than are sufficient to employ that portion of life which any mere reader and recipient of poetical impressions should devote to them, and these having been produced in poetical times, are far superior in all the characteristics of poetry to the artificial reconstructions of a few morbid ascetics in unpoetical times. To read the promiscuous rubbish of the present time to the exclusion of the select treasures of the past, is to substitute the worse for the better variety of the same mode of enjoyment.

But in whatever degree poetry is cultivated, it must necessarily be to the neglect of some branch of useful study: and it is a lamentable spectacle to see minds, capable of better things, running to seed in the specious indolence of these empty aimless mockeries of intellectual exertion. Poetry was the mental rattle that awakened the attention of intellect in the infancy of civil society: but for the maturity of mind to make a serious business of the playthings of its childhood, is as absurd as for a full-grown man to rub his gums with coral, and cry to be charmed to sleep by the jingle of silver bells.

As to that small portion of our contemporary poetry, which is neither descriptive, nor narrative, nor dramatic, and which, for want of a better name, may be called ethical, the most distinguished portion of it, consisting merely of querulous, egotistical rhapsodies, to express the writer's high dissatisfaction with the world and everything in it, serves only to confirm what has been said of the semi-barbarous character of poets, who from singing dithyrambics and "Io Triumphe," while society was savage, grow rabid, and out of their element, as it becomes polished and enlightened.

Now when we consider that it is not to the thinking and studious, and scientific and philosophical part of the community, not to those whose minds are bent on the pursuit and promotion of permanently useful ends and aims, that poets must address their minstrelsy, but to that much larger portion of the reading public, whose minds are not awakened to the desire of valuable knowledge, and who are indifferent to anything beyond being charmed, moved, excited, affected, and exalted; charmed by harmony, moved by sentiment, excited by passion, affected by pathos, and exalted by sublimity; harmony, which is language on the rack of Procrustes; sentiment, which is canting egotism in the mask of refined feeling; passion, which is the commotion of a weak and selfish mind; pathos, which is the whining of an unmanly spirit; and sublimity, which is the inflation of an empty head: when we consider that the great and permanent interests of human society become more and more the main-spring of intellectual pursuit; that in proportion as they become so, the subordinacy of the ornamental to the useful will be more and more seen and acknowledged, and that therefore the progress of useful art and science, and of moral and political knowledge, will continue more and more to withdraw attention from frivolous and unconducive, to solid and conducive studies: that therefore the poetical audience will not only continually diminish in the proportion of its number to that of the rest of the reading public, but will also sink lower and lower in the comparison of intellectual acquirement: when we consider that the poet must still please his audience, and must therefore continue to sink to their level, while the rest of the community is rising above it: we may easily conceive that the day is not distant, when the degraded state of every species of poetry will be as generally recognized as that of dramatic poetry has long been: and this not from any decrease either of intellectual power, or intellectual acquisition, but because intellectual power and intellectual acquisition have turned themselves into other and better channels, and have abandoned the cultivation and the fate of poetry to the degenerate fry of modern rhymesters, and their olympic judges, the magazine critics, who continue to debate and promulgate oracles about poetry, as if it were still what it was in the Homeric age, the all-in-all of intellectual progression, and as if there were no such things in existence as mathematicians, astronomers, chemists, moralists, metaphysicians, historians, politicians, and political economists, who have built into the upper air of intelligence a pyramid, from the summit of which they see the modern Parnassus far beneath them, and, knowing how small a place it occupies in the comprehensiveness of their prospect, smile at the little ambition and the circumscribed perceptions with which the drivellers and mountebanks upon it are contending for the poetical palm and the critical chair.

Thomas Love Peacock, "The Four Ages of Poetry," *The Works of Percy Bysshe Shelley*, ed. H. Buxton Forman (London: Reeves and Turner, 1880), VII, 386–404.

Selected Bibliography

EDITIONS

The Works of Percy Bysshe Shelley. Ed. H. Buxton Forman. 8 vols. London: Reeves, 1880.

PERCY BYSSHE SHELLEY. *A Defense of Poetry.* Ed. A. S. Cook. Boston: Ginn and Company, 1890.

The Complete Poetical Works of Percy Bysshe Shelley. Ed. Thomas Hutchinson. London: Oxford University Press, 1904. New edition, with introduction and notes by Benjamin P. Kurtz, 1933.

Shelley's Literary and Philosophical Criticism. Ed. John Shawcross. London: Oxford University Press, 1909.

The Letters of Percy Bysshe Shelley. Ed. Roger Ingpen. 2 vols. London: Sir Isaac Pitman and Sons, Ltd., 1909. Revised, 1915, with some additional letters.

Shelley's Prose in the Bodleian Manuscripts. Ed. Andre H. Koszul. London: Oxford University Press, 1910.

Shelley's Defence of Poetry and Browning's Essay on Shelley. Ed. L. Winstanley. Boston and London: D. C. Heath, 1911.

Peacock's Four Ages of Poetry, Shelley's Defence of Poetry, Browning's Essay on Shelley. Ed. H. F. B. Brett-Smith. Boston: Houghton Mifflin Co., 1921.

The Complete Works of Percy Bysshe Shelley. Ed. Roger Ingpen and Walter E. Peck. Julian Edition. 10 vols. New York: Charles Scribner's Sons, 1926–1930. Reissued, Brooklyn, N.Y.: The Gordian Press, 1965.

Shelley's Prose: Or the Trumpet of Prophecy. Ed. David Lee Clark. Albuquerque: University of New Mexico Press, 1954.

The Letters of Percy Bysshe Shelley. Ed. F. L. Jones. 2 vols. Oxford: Oxford University Press, 1964.

BIOGRAPHY AND CRITICISM

ABRAMS, M. H. *The Mirror and the Lamp: Romantic Theory and the Critical Tradition.* New York: Oxford University Press, 1953. Reissued, W. W. Norton and Company, 1958.

BAKER, JOSEPH E. *Shelley's Platonic Answer to a Platonic Attack.* Iowa City: University of Iowa Press, 1965.

BRADLEY, ANDREW C. "Shelley's View of Poetry." In *Oxford Lectures on Poetry.* London: Macmillan, 1909.

CAMERON, KENNETH NEILL. *The Young Shelley.* New York: Macmillan, 1950.

CLUTTON-BROCK, ARTHUR. *Shelley: The Man and the Poet.* New York: Dutton, 1909.

DOWDEN, EDWARD. *The Life of P. B. Shelley.* 2 vols. London: Kegan Paul, 1886.

ELIOT, T. S. "Shelley and Keats." In *The Use of Poetry and the Use of Criticism.* Cambridge: Harvard University Press, 1933.

ELTON, OLIVER. *A Survey of English Literature, 1780–1830.* 2 vols. New York: Macmillan, 1912.

LEWIS, C. S. "Shelley, Dryden, and Mr. Eliot." In *Rehabilitations.* London: Oxford University Press, 1939.

MCELDERRY, B. R., JR. "Common Elements in Wordsworth's 'Preface' and Shelley's *Defence of Poetry,*" *Modern Language Quarterly,* V (June 1944), 175–181.

MORE, PAUL ELMER. "Shelley." In *Shelburne Essays: Seventh Series.* Boston: Houghton Mifflin, 1910.

NOTOPOULOS, JAMES A. *The Platonism of Shelley.* Durham: Duke University Press, 1949.

PECK, WALTER E. *Shelley, His Life and Works.* 2 vols. Boston: Houghton Mifflin, 1927.

POTTLE, FREDERICK A. "The Case of Shelley," *PMLA,* LXVII (September 1952), 589–608.

READ, HERBERT. *In Defence of Shelley and Other Essays.* London: Heinemann, 1936.

SWINBURNE, A. C. "Notes on the Text of Shelley," *Essays and Studies.* London: Chatto & Windus, 1875.

TINKER, CHAUNCEY B. "Shelley Once More," *Yale Review,* XXXI (September 1941), 87–94.

VERKOREN, LUCAS. *A Study of Shelley's "Defence of Poetry."* Amsterdam: F. Mijis, 1937.

Wasserman, Earl R. "Shelley's Last Poetics: A Reconsideration." In *From Sensibility to Romanticism*, ed. F. W. Hilles and H. Bloom. New York: Oxford University Press, 1965.

———. *Shelley's Prometheus Unbound*. Baltimore: The Johns Hopkins University Press, 1965.

Weaver, Bennett. "Shelley." In *The English Romantic Poets: A Review of Research*, ed. Thomas M. Raysor. New York: Modern Language Association, 1950.

White, Newman Ivey. *Shelley*. 2 vols. New York: Knopf, 1940.

———. *Portrait of Shelley*. New York: Knopf, 1945.

Yeats, William Butler. "The Philosophy of Shelley." In *Ideas of Good and Evil*. Stratford-on-Avon: Shakespeare Head Press, 1908. Essay first appeared in 1900.

Acknowledgments

Thanks are due to the Gordian Press, Brooklyn, N.Y., for permission to reprint from the Julian Edition of Shelley's "A Defence of Poetry," Shelley's prefaces, and his reviews.

Mr. Robert H. Holland of Sir Isaac Pitman and Sons, Ltd., Mr. John Murray, and Professor Frederick L. Jones of the University of Pennsylvania have kindly answered queries regarding Shelley's letters.

To the Huntington Library and to the British Museum I am grateful for the opportunity to compare original editions of Shelley's works with later editions.

My colleague, Professor Edward N. O'Neil, of the Classics Department of the University of Southern California, has helped me with many of the Greek and Latin passages. My wife, Frances, has as usual shared in assembling the materials and reading both manuscript and proofs.

The Research Fund of the College of Letters, Arts, and Sciences has provided various study materials.

Finally, I wish to thank Professor Paul A. Olson, Editor of the Regents Critics Series, for many helpful suggestions in the revision of the original manuscript.

BRUCE R. MCELDERRY, JR.

Index